Collins

White Rose Maths
AQA GCSE 9-1 Revision Guide

Aiming for Grade 7/8/9

Series editor: Ian Davies
Authors: Matthew Ainscough, Simon Bond, Robert Clasper, Ian Davies, Emily Fox, James Hunter, Rhys Jowett and Sahar Shillabeer

Published by Collins
An imprint of HarperCollins*Publishers*
1 London Bridge Street
London SE1 9GF

HarperCollins*Publishers*
1st Floor, Watermarque Building,
Ringsend Road, Dublin 4, Ireland

ISBN: 978-0-00-853244-4

First published 2022

10 9 8 7 6 5 4 3 2 1

British Library Cataloguing in Publication Data.

A CIP record of this book is available from the British Library.

Series editor: Ian Davies
Authors: Matthew Ainscough, Simon Bond, Robert Clasper, Ian Davies, Emily Fox, James Hunter, Rhys Jowett and Sahar Shillabeer
Publishers: Katie Sergeant and Clare Souza
Project management and editorial: Richard Toms and Amanda Dickson
Inside concept design: Ian Wrigley
Typesetting: Nicola Lancashire (Rose and Thorn Creative Services)
Cover design: Sarah Duxbury
Production: Lyndsey Rogers
Printed in the United Kingdom by Martins the Printers

MIX
Paper from
responsible source

FSC www.fsc.org **FSC® C007454**

This book is produced from independently certified FSC™ paper
to ensure responsible forest management.

For more information visit: www.harpercollins.co.uk/green

Contents

Introduction

How to use this revision guide

Welcome to the *Collins White Rose Maths AQA GCSE 9–1 Revision Guide – Aiming for Grade 7/8/9*. In this guide, you will revisit all the key topics you need to know and get plenty of practice to reinforce the knowledge, skills and understanding you need. The guide is suitable if you are sitting Higher tier with a target grade of 7, 8 or 9.

We hope you enjoy your learning journey. Here is a short guide to how to get the most out of this book.

Inside a unit

At the start of each section, there are some basics you should already know if you are aiming for a grade 7, 8 or 9. Key facts and practice questions are provided for each of these topics. If you are not sure about this material, you will find support in the *Collins White Rose Maths AQA GCSE 9–1 Revision Guide – Aiming for Grade 5/6* (ISBN 978-0-00-853243-7). After this, each topic is covered on a double page with everything you need to know and material for you to practise.

Facts

The 'Facts' part reminds you about what you need to know about each topic in order to succeed. This includes models and diagrams to support your understanding and definitions of key words.

Foundations

A few questions to make sure you know the basics you need to be able to do well at this topic. These are covered in detail in earlier books in this series, such as the *Collins White Rose Maths AQA GCSE 9–1 Revision Guide – Aiming for Grade 5/6*.

Focus

The 'Focus' part gives you worked examples on the topic you're revising. Alongside a step-by-step solution that models how you would answer exam questions, there is a detailed commentary which explains the working.

Many of the units in this guide can be tackled without a calculator, but feel free to use one to support you when you need to. Keep both your number and your calculator skills sharp by working both ways and checking your answers whenever you can.

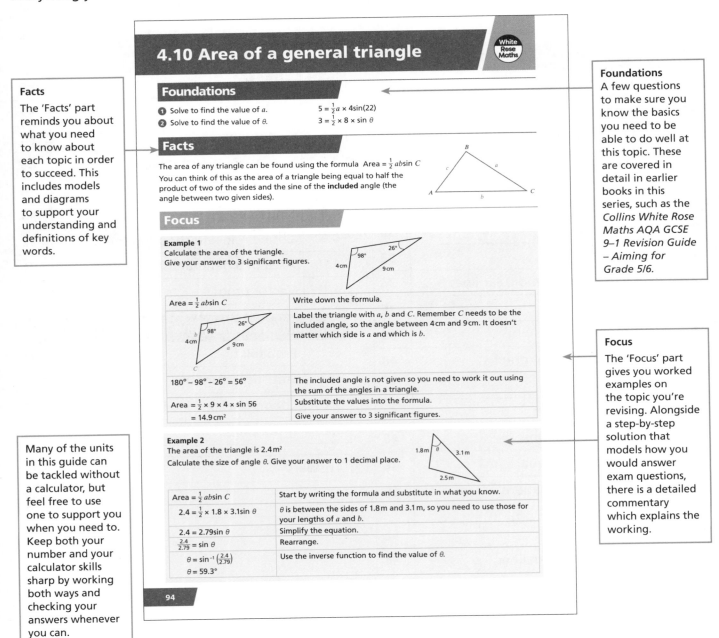

4

Section 5 – Probability and Statistics

Fluency

1. The masses of 100 apples in an orchard are recorded in the table.

Mass, m (g)	$0 < m \leqslant 25$	$25 < m \leqslant 40$	$40 < m \leqslant 60$	$60 < m \leqslant 75$	$75 < m \leqslant 100$
Frequency	12	15	25	33	15

Draw a histogram to show this information.

2. The table shows information about the scores of some students in an assessment.

Score, s	$0 < s \leqslant 120$	$120 < s \leqslant 200$	$200 < s \leqslant 300$	$300 < s \leqslant 450$	$450 < s \leqslant 500$
Frequency	24	18	15	24	6

a) Draw a histogram to show this information.

b) Estimate the number of students who scored less than 250 marks.

> Think about the area of the bars and parts of bars that show scores $0 < s < 250$

3. This histogram shows information about the masses of some cats and kittens at a shelter.

a) Use the histogram to complete the table below.

Mass, m (kg)	$0 < m \leqslant 1.5$	$1.5 < m \leqslant 3$	$3 < m \leqslant 4$	$4 < m \leqslant 6$
Frequency				

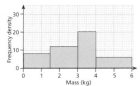

b) Estimate the number of cats with mass greater than 3.5 kg.

Further

1. The incomplete histogram and table below give information about the ages of customers in a supermarket.

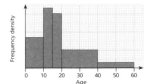

Age, a (years)	Frequency
$0 < a \leqslant 10$	34
$10 < a \leqslant 15$	33
$15 < a \leqslant 20$	
$20 < a \leqslant 40$	
$40 < a \leqslant 60$	

Use the histogram to complete the table of values.　(4 marks)

2. The table shows information about the times taken by some students to run 60 m.

Time, t (s)	$10 < t \leqslant 12$	$12 < t \leqslant 14$	$14 < t \leqslant 16$	$16 < t \leqslant 17$	$17 < t \leqslant 20$
Frequency	8	12	10		9

a) Use the table to complete the histogram.　(3 marks)

b) Use the histogram to complete the missing entry in the table.　(1 mark)

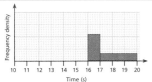

> You will need separate sheets of paper, including graph paper, to complete the questions in the 'Fluency' and 'Further' parts.

Histograms　105

If you are confident with everything in this guide, you should be well on your way to your target grade of 7, 8 or 9 in GCSE mathematics.

Good luck with your studying and your examinations!

Ian Davies

Series Editor

Facts

Equivalent fractions have the same value and can be found by multiplying or dividing the numerator and denominator of the fraction by the same number.

$$\frac{2}{3} = \frac{16}{24} \quad (\times 8)$$

$$\frac{25}{40} = \frac{5}{8} \quad (\div 5)$$

Writing fractions as tenths, hundredths, thousandths, etc. helps to **convert them to decimals**.

$$\frac{3}{5} = \frac{6}{10} = 0.6 \quad (\times 2)$$

$$\frac{143}{200} = \frac{715}{1000} = 0.715 \quad (\times 5)$$

You can also use **division**.

$$\frac{3}{8} = 3 \div 8$$

$$8 \overline{\smash{)}3 \cdot {}^{3}0 \; {}^{6}0 \; {}^{4}0} \quad = 0.375$$

You can also convert decimals to fractions.

$$0.475 = \frac{475}{1000} = \frac{95}{200} = \frac{19}{40} \quad (\div 5)(\div 5)$$

To add or subtract fractions, use equivalent fractions to find a common denominator and then add (or subtract) the numerators: $\frac{5}{6} + \frac{3}{4} = \frac{10}{12} + \frac{9}{12} = \frac{19}{12} = 1\frac{7}{12}$

To multiply fractions, you multiply the numerators and multiply the denominators: $\frac{3}{5} \times \frac{4}{7} = \frac{12}{35}$

Look for factors to make the calculations easier: $\frac{7}{12_4}^{1} \times \frac{9^3}{14_2} = \frac{3}{8}$

The **reciprocal** of a fraction is found by swapping the numerator and denominator.
For example, the reciprocal of $\frac{3}{5}$ is $\frac{5}{3}$. Notice that the product of a fraction and its reciprocal is always 1
$\frac{3}{5} \times \frac{5}{3} = \frac{15}{15} = 1$

To **divide by a fraction**, you multiply by its reciprocal.
$\frac{3}{5} \div \frac{2}{9} = \frac{3}{5} \times \frac{9}{2} = \frac{27}{10} = 2\frac{7}{10}$

A **percentage** such as 45% (read as 'forty-five percent') is a number of parts per hundred. A percentage can be represented as a fraction ($\frac{45}{100}$ which simplifies to $\frac{9}{20}$) or as a decimal (0.45, the result of 45 ÷ 100).

There are many ways to **calculate percentages of amounts**.

For example, to find 45% of 60 you could:

- find 50% (60 ÷ 2 = 30), find 5% (50% ÷ 10 = 30 ÷ 10 = 3) and subtract (45% = 50% − 5% = 30 − 3 = 27)
- find 1% (60 ÷ 100) and multiply the answer by 45
- use the fraction multiplication $\frac{45}{100} \times 60$
- use a **decimal multiplier** by working out 0.45 × 60; this is the most efficient way if you have a calculator, especially when working with more challenging percentages such as 37% or 1.6%

To **express one amount as a percentage of another**, you can:

- express as a fraction and convert; for example, a mark of 24 out of 60 as a percentage is $\frac{24}{60} = \frac{2}{5} = \frac{4}{10} = 40\%$
- divide and convert the decimal if you have a calculator; for example, if 6 out of 32 students are absent, then 6 ÷ 32 = 0.1875 = 18.75% ≈ 19%

To increase or decrease by a percentage, the most efficient method is to use a decimal multiplier. For example, if a salary of £40 000 is increased by 6%, you would have 106%, so work out 1.06 × £40 000 Likewise, if the salary is decreased by 2.5%, you would have 97.5%, so work out 0.975 × £40 000

This is particularly useful when dealing with **repeated percentage change**. For example, if a population of 60 000 decreases by 12% a year for three successive years, the final population can be found by working out 60 000 × 0.88 × 0.88 × 0.88, or 60 000 × 0.88³

Repeated multiplication like this uses **powers** or **indices**, for example $3^4 = 3 \times 3 \times 3 \times 3 = 81$. To find out more about working with numbers involving indices, including **standard form**, see unit 2F1.

Practice

1 Put these values in order of size, starting with the smallest:

    a) $0.4, \frac{3}{8}, 38\%$ b) $\frac{5}{6}, 0.805, 82\%, \frac{17}{20}$

2 Work out the answers to these calculations, giving your answers in their simplest form.

    a) $\frac{4}{5} + \frac{2}{3}$ b) $\frac{4}{5} \times \frac{2}{3}$ c) $\frac{4}{5} - \frac{2}{3}$ d) $\frac{4}{5} \div \frac{2}{3}$

3 a) $5\frac{2}{3} - 2\frac{1}{4}$ b) $3\frac{5}{8} + 7\frac{5}{6}$

    c) $6\frac{2}{3} \times 2\frac{1}{5}$ d) $6\frac{2}{3} \div 2$ | To multiply and divide mixed numbers, you need to convert them to improper fractions first. |

    e) $6\frac{2}{3} \div \frac{1}{2}$ f) $6\frac{2}{3} \div 2\frac{1}{2}$

4 $\frac{4}{5}$ of a number is 600

Work out $\frac{2}{3}$ of the number. | Draw a bar model. |

5 Complete the table of equivalences.

Percentage	Fraction	Decimal
8%		
		0.3
		0.03
2.5%		
	$\frac{11}{200}$	

6 Without using a calculator, work out:

    a) 25% of 60 kg   b) 30% of 800 g   c) 90% of 50 m

    d) 75% of £12 000   e) 120% of 80 cm   f) 350% of £80

7 Use a calculator to work out:

    a) 73% of 90 kg   b) 31% of £750   c) 17% of 600 ml   d) 28% of £9000

    e) 9.6% of £4000   f) 1.2% of 30 kg   g) 128.7% of £800   h) 210.67% of 8 km

8 Emily buys a house for £280 000

She sells the house for £257 600

Calculate the percentage loss she makes.

9 Amina invests £30 000 at a rate of 1.7% interest per annum.

    a) How much will her investment be worth after:

        i) 1 year?   ii) 2 years?   iii) 3 years?

    b) How much interest will Amina earn in 5 years?

10 A number is increased by 30% and the result deceased by 30%

What percentage of the original number is the final answer? Choose the correct option.

70%   91%   100%   121%

1.1 Estimating powers and roots

Foundations

1 Write down the values of:

   a) 4^2 b) 7^2 c) 8^2 d) 9^2 e) 11^2 f) 12^2 g) 2^3 h) 5^3 i) 6^3

2 Write down the values of:

   a) $\sqrt{25}$ b) $\sqrt{100}$ c) $\sqrt{196}$ d) $\sqrt[3]{27}$ e) $\sqrt[3]{64}$

Facts

You can **estimate** powers of numbers by considering the powers of the closest integers to the number.

Roots can be estimated by considering roots that have integer values which are above and below the number that you are trying to find the root of.

You can use a **number line** to help your reasoning:

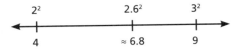

This number line shows that $2.6^2 \approx 6.8$ using the fact that $2^2 = 4$ and $3^2 = 9$

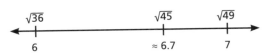

This number line shows that $\sqrt{45} \approx 6.7$ using the fact that $\sqrt{36} = 6$ and $\sqrt{49} = 7$

Focus

Example 1

Estimate the value of 5.8^2

$5^2 = 25$ and $6^2 = 36$	Write down the squares of the closest integers above and below 5.8
[number line: 5^2 at 25, $5.8^2 \approx 34$, 6^2 at 36]	You may wish to use a number line to help you visualise your estimate.
$5.8^2 \approx 34$ You should use the approximately equal to sign ($\approx$) to show that your solution is an approximation.	5.8 is closer to 6 than 5 so the square of 5.8 will be closer to 36 than to 25

Example 2

Estimate the value of $\sqrt[3]{20}$

$\sqrt[3]{8} = 2$ and $\sqrt[3]{27} = 3$	Considering the cube roots of numbers above and below 20 that give integer values, you can find that $\sqrt[3]{20}$ is greater than 2 and less than 3
[number line: $\sqrt[3]{8}$ at 2, $\sqrt[3]{20} \approx 2.7$, $\sqrt[3]{27}$ at 3]	20 is closer to 27 than 8 so the cube root of 20 will be closer to 3 than to 2
$\sqrt[3]{20} \approx 2.7$	

Example 3

Estimate the value of $\sqrt{0.5}$

$\sqrt{0.5} \approx \sqrt{0.49}$	You may notice that the root that you are trying to estimate is close to a root that can be evaluated mentally.
$\sqrt{49} = 7$ So $\sqrt{0.49} = 0.7$	You can use known integer roots to deduce decimal roots.
$\sqrt{0.5} \approx 0.71$	As 0.5 is slightly greater than 0.49, the root will be slightly more than 0.7

Fluency

1 Estimate the value of: a) 2.3^2 b) 8.6^2 c) 5.5^2 d) 2.3^3

2 Estimate the value of: a) $\sqrt{18}$ b) $\sqrt{92}$ c) $\sqrt{130}$ d) $\sqrt[3]{73}$

3 Estimate the value of: a) $\sqrt{0.8}$ b) $\sqrt{0.15}$ c) $\sqrt{1.45}$ d) $\sqrt[3]{0.063}$

4 Estimate the value of $\sqrt{1620}$ | You could use the fact that $\sqrt{16} = 4$ to consider $\sqrt{1600}$ and use this to help you find the estimate.

5 Estimate the value of: a) 3.7^4 b) 2.9^5 c) 1.7^6

Further

1 Use <, > or = to complete the statement. Justify your answer.   (2 marks)

$\sqrt{10}$ .... $\sqrt[3]{26}$

2 Write the following in order of size, starting with the smallest.   (2 marks)

   10          $\sqrt{103}$ 3.1^2 1.9^3 9

3 Mario says, "I know that $\sqrt{64}$ is equal to 8 so $\sqrt{32}$ must be equal to 4."

   a) Explain Mario's mistake.   (1 mark)

   b) Work out a more suitable estimate of $\sqrt{32}$ (2 marks)

4 Estimate the value of $\sqrt{3.4^2 + 13 \times 4.8}$ (3 marks)

1.2 Fractional indices

Foundations

1 Write down the value of:

   a) 3^4 **b)** 3^2 **c)** 3^1 **d)** 10^9 **e)** 10^3 **f)** 10^1

2 Write down the value of:

   a) $\sqrt{144}$ **b)** $\sqrt{400}$ **c)** $\sqrt[3]{27}$ **d)** $\sqrt[3]{125}$ **e)** $\sqrt[4]{81}$

Facts

When you apply the multiplication rule for indices, you can see that:

$a^{\frac{1}{2}} \times a^{\frac{1}{2}} = a^1$, therefore $a^{\frac{1}{2}} = \sqrt{a}$

Similarly, $a^{\frac{1}{3}} \times a^{\frac{1}{3}} \times a^{\frac{1}{3}} = a^1$, therefore $a^{\frac{1}{3}} = \sqrt[3]{a}$

You can then generalise to give $a^{\frac{1}{n}} = \sqrt[n]{a}$

Then, using the knowledge that $(a^b)^c = a^{bc}$, you can further generalise to give:

$$a^{\frac{m}{n}} = \left(a^{\frac{1}{n}}\right)^m$$

$$= \left(\sqrt[n]{a}\right)^m$$

> Alternatively, you could express $a^{\frac{m}{n}}$ as $(a^m)^{\frac{1}{n}} = \sqrt[n]{a^m}$
> However, it is usually easier to apply the root first.

Also, since $a^{-p} = \frac{1}{a^p}$, you can also have negative fractional indices where $a^{-\frac{m}{n}} = \frac{1}{\left(\sqrt[n]{a}\right)^m}$

Focus

Example 1

Work out the value of $49^{\frac{1}{2}}$

$49^{\frac{1}{2}} = \sqrt{49}$ $= 7$	Recognise that $a^{\frac{1}{n}} = \sqrt[n]{a}$

Example 2

Work out the value of $81^{\frac{3}{4}}$

$81^{\frac{3}{4}} = \left(81^{\frac{1}{4}}\right)^3 = \left(\sqrt[4]{81}\right)^3$ $= 3^3$ $= 27$	Recognise that $a^{\frac{m}{n}} = \left(a^{\frac{1}{n}}\right)^m$ You could have cubed 81 and then taken the fourth root of your answer. That method would be inefficient and you may not recognise that $531\,441 = 27^4$

Example 3

$125^n = \frac{1}{25}$

Work out the value of n.

$(5^3)^n = \frac{1}{5^2}$	Recognise that 125 and 25 are both powers of 5
$5^{3n} = 5^{-2}$	Write both sides of the equation as a single power of 5
$3n = -2$ $n = -\frac{2}{3}$	Since the bases are equal, the indices must also be equal, so you can form and solve an equation.

Fluency

① Evaluate:

a) $36^{\frac{1}{2}}$

b) $100^{\frac{1}{2}}$

c) $64^{\frac{1}{3}}$

d) $27^{\frac{1}{3}}$

e) $1^{\frac{1}{5}}$

f) $\left(\frac{1}{9}\right)^{\frac{1}{2}}$

g) $\left(\frac{1}{8}\right)^{\frac{1}{3}}$

h) $\left(\frac{1}{32}\right)^{\frac{1}{5}}$

i) $\left(\frac{9}{16}\right)^{\frac{1}{2}}$

j) $\left(\frac{125}{64}\right)^{\frac{1}{3}}$

② Find the value of:

a) $8^{\frac{2}{3}}$

b) $16^{\frac{3}{2}}$

c) $4^{\frac{5}{2}}$

d) $216^{\frac{2}{3}}$

e) $125^{\frac{4}{3}}$

f) $\left(\frac{1}{16}\right)^{\frac{3}{4}}$

g) $\left(\frac{4}{25}\right)^{\frac{3}{2}}$

h) $\left(\frac{64}{27}\right)^{\frac{2}{3}}$

③ Write each of the following in the form $\frac{a}{b}$ where a and b are integers.

a) $49^{-\frac{1}{2}}$

b) $27^{-\frac{2}{3}}$

c) $\left(\frac{25}{36}\right)^{-\frac{3}{2}}$

d) $\left(\frac{64}{125}\right)^{-\frac{2}{3}}$

④ $8^{2n} = 2^{18}$

Circle the value of n.

1.5   3   6   9

Further

① $4 \times \sqrt{8} = 2^n$

Work out the value of n.   (3 marks)

② Aaliyah says $16^{\frac{3}{2}} = 24$

a) Explain the mistake that Aaliyah has made.   (1 mark)

b) Work out the value of $16^{\frac{3}{2}}$ (2 marks)

③ Solve $m^{\frac{4}{3}} = 81$ (2 marks)

④ $\dfrac{1}{(16^5)^{\frac{1}{3}}} = 2^n$

Work out the value of n.   (2 marks)

1.3 Upper and lower bounds

Foundations

1 Round each number to 2 significant figures.

a) 274.9   b) 275   c) 284   d) 284.9   e) 284.99   f) 285

2 Round each number to 1 decimal place.

a) 2.449   b) 2.45   c) 2.503   d) 2.549   e) 2.54999   f) 2.55

Facts

When you use a measurement, it is never totally accurate. For example, if your height was given as 155 cm, you would be very unlikely to be exactly 155 cm tall. You could be 154.7 cm or 155.34 cm, for example.

You can use bounds to consider what the least and greatest values are when given a degree of accuracy.

For example, if the length of a train carriage is 22 m to the nearest metre, it could be as short as 21.5 m and as long as any length up to but not including 22.5 m. This can be shown on a number line.

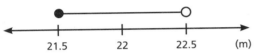

| 21.5 | 22 | 22.5 | (m) |

If the length of the train was 22.5 m, this would round to 23 m. For this reason, we often use inequalities to write upper and lower bounds. These are often called error intervals. For this example, the error interval for the length would be $21.5 \leqslant l < 22.5$

You may need to use multiple upper and lower bounds to find the upper and lower bounds of the results of calculations. You can work out bounds for numbers that have been rounded or truncated.

Focus

Example 1

A watch has a mass of 150 grams rounded to the nearest gram.

Write the upper bound and the lower bound for the mass of the watch.

Lower bound = 149.5 g Upper bound = 150.5 g	The lower bound is the least possible mass. It is important to recognise that this is the upper bound. If the watch was 150.5 g, it would round to 151 g to the nearest gram. For many questions, the level of accuracy can be halved then added to or subtracted from the rounded value.

Example 2

The diagram shows a rectangle.

The measurements have been truncated to 2 significant figures.

Write the error interval for the area of the rectangle.

11 cm   14 cm

Length Upper bound = 15 Lower bound = 14	Width Upper bound = 12 Lower bound = 11	Work out the upper and lower bounds for the length and width of the rectangle. Remember that truncation is different from rounding.

A_{upper} = 15 × 12
       = 180 cm²
A_{lower} = 14 × 11
       = 154 cm²
		To find the greatest possible area, you need to use the upper bound of both the length and the width.
		
		To find the least possible area, you need to use the lower bound of both the length and the width.

154 cm² $\leqslant A <$ 180 cm²		You need to write the error interval as an inequality.

Example 3

$a = \frac{b}{c-d}$ $b = 6$ to the nearest integer $c = 3.2$ to 1 decimal place $d = 1.7$ to 1 decimal place

Work out the upper bound for a. Give your answer to 1 decimal place.

$b_{lower} = 5.5$ $c_{lower} = 3.15$ $d_{lower} = 1.65$	$b_{upper} = 6.5$ $c_{upper} = 3.25$ $d_{upper} = 1.75$	First you should find the upper and lower bounds for b, c and d.
$a_{upper} = \dfrac{b_{upper}}{(c-d)_{lower}}$ $= \dfrac{b_{upper}}{c_{lower} - d_{upper}}$ $= \dfrac{6.5}{3.15 - 1.75}$ $= 4.6$ (1 d.p.)		To find the upper bound of a, you need to use the upper bound of b and the lower bound of $c - d$. To find the lower bound of $c - d$, you need to use the lower bound of c and the upper bound of d.

Fluency

1. Five pieces of wood each measure 2.8 m correct to the nearest 10 cm. Work out:
   a) the lower bound for the total length of the five pieces of wood
   b) the upper bound for the total length of the five pieces of wood

2. $v = \frac{b}{n}$

   $b = 180$ correct to 2 significant figures $n = 4.93$ correct to 3 significant figures

   Work out the lower bound for v. Give your answer to 3 significant figures.

3. $q = \frac{w}{k-t}$

   $w = 13.2$ correct to 1 decimal place

   $k = 4.36$ correct to 3 significant figures

   $t = 0.42$ correct to 2 significant figures

   Work out the value of q, giving your answer to a suitable degree of accuracy. Explain your reasoning.

Further

1. Filipo ran 500 m to the nearest 10 m. The time for the run was 1 minute and 13 seconds to the nearest second. Work out:
   a) the upper bound for Filipo's average speed   (2 marks)
   b) the lower bound for Filipo's average speed   (2 marks)
   Give your answers in metres per second.

2. A circle has an area of 150 cm² correct to 2 significant figures.

   Work out the upper and lower bounds for the radius of the circle. Give your answer to 2 significant figures.   (3 marks)

3. Triangle ABC is shown.

   The length is given correct to the nearest centimetre.

   The angle is given correct to the nearest 1 degree.

   Work out the lower bound for the length AC, giving your answer to 3 significant figures.   (3 marks)

   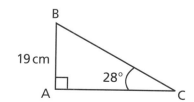

4. A cylindrical tank has a radius of 0.8 m truncated to 1 decimal place and a height of 1 m truncated to 1 significant figure.

   The tank is filled with water using a bucket with a capacity of 10 litres correct to the nearest litre.

   Work out the upper bound for the number of buckets of water used to completely fill the tank.   (4 marks)

1.4 Simplifying surd expressions and rationalising denominators

Foundations

1 List the factors of:

　　a) 48　　　　　　b) 80　　　　c) 32

2 List:

　　a) the first 15 square numbers　　　　b) the first five cube numbers

Facts

A **surd** is a number that cannot be simplified to remove root symbols, such as $\sqrt{}$ or $\sqrt[3]{}$

To simplify surds, you can use the general rules for multiplication and division:

$$\sqrt{a} \times \sqrt{b} = \sqrt{ab}$$

$$\frac{\sqrt{a}}{\sqrt{b}} = \sqrt{\frac{a}{b}}$$

$$\sqrt{a} \times \sqrt{a} = a$$

There are no similar rules for addition and subtraction, but you can add and subtract 'like surds' the same way as like algebraic terms. For example, $3\sqrt{5} + 4\sqrt{5} = 7\sqrt{5}$

> You may be able to add or subtract two surds where the numbers in the roots are not the same if you can simplify the surd to make the numbers in the root equal.

Surds are **irrational** and so cannot be written in the form $\frac{a}{b}$ where a and b are integers. However, if you have a fraction with a denominator that is a surd, you can simplify it by **rationalising the denominator**. If the denominator is in the form $\sqrt{n}$, you need to multiply both the numerator and denominator by $\sqrt{n}$. If the denominator is in the form $a + \sqrt{b}$, you need to multiply them both by $a - \sqrt{b}$.

Focus

Example 1

Simplify $\sqrt{80}$

$\sqrt{80} = \sqrt{16} \times \sqrt{5}$	Identify the greatest square factor of 80 and express the surd as a product using $\sqrt{a} \times \sqrt{b} = \sqrt{ab}$
$= 4 \times \sqrt{5}$ $= 4\sqrt{5}$	Evaluate the square root and rewrite the surd without using the multiplication symbol.

Example 2

Simplify $(7 + \sqrt{8})(11 - \sqrt{2})$, giving your answer in the form $a + b\sqrt{2}$ where a and b are integers.

$(7 + \sqrt{8})(11 - \sqrt{2}) = 77 + 11\sqrt{8} - 7\sqrt{2} - \sqrt{16}$	Expand the double bracket.
$= 77 + 11 \times \sqrt{4} \times \sqrt{2} - 7\sqrt{2} - 4$	Express $\sqrt{8}$ in the form $\sqrt{4} \times \sqrt{2}$ and evaluate $\sqrt{16}$
$= 77 + 22\sqrt{2} - 7\sqrt{2} - 4$	Simplify the second term.
$= 73 + 15\sqrt{2}$	Collect like terms.

Example 3

a) Rewrite $\frac{6}{\sqrt{3}}$ with a rational denominator.

b) Write $\frac{7 - \sqrt{20}}{4 + \sqrt{5}}$ in the form $\frac{a + b\sqrt{c}}{d}$ where a, b, c and d are integers.

a) $\frac{6}{\sqrt{3}} \times \frac{\sqrt{3}}{\sqrt{3}} = \frac{6\sqrt{3}}{3} = 2\sqrt{3}$	To rationalise the denominator, multiply the numerator and denominator by $\sqrt{3}$ and then simplify.
b) $\frac{7 - \sqrt{20}}{4 + \sqrt{5}} \times \frac{4 - \sqrt{5}}{4 - \sqrt{5}} = \frac{28 - 7\sqrt{5} - 4\sqrt{20} + \sqrt{100}}{16 + 4\sqrt{5} - 4\sqrt{5} - 5}$	Recognise the form of the denominator and multiply by $4 - \sqrt{5}$
$= \frac{28 - 7\sqrt{5} - 8\sqrt{5} + 10}{16 - 5}$	Simplify the numerator and denominator. You may need to use a combination of surd rules.
$= \frac{38 - 15\sqrt{5}}{11}$	Your calculator display will give a surd in its simplest form.

Fluency

1. Write in simplest surd form.

   a) $\sqrt{75}$ b) $\sqrt{300}$ c) $\sqrt{250}$ d) $\sqrt{72}$ e) $\sqrt{48}$

2. Chloe is simplifying $\sqrt{800}$. Her working is below.

   $\sqrt{800} = \sqrt{4} \times \sqrt{200}$
   $= 2\sqrt{200}$

   a) Explain why Chloe can further simplify the surd.

   b) Express $\sqrt{800}$ in the form $a\sqrt{2}$ where a is an integer.

3. Express $\sqrt{20} + \sqrt{45}$ in the form $a\sqrt{b}$ where a and b are integers.

4. Express $5\sqrt{108} - 3\sqrt{12}$ in the form $a\sqrt{b}$ where a and b are integers.

5. Rationalise the denominator of $\frac{8}{\sqrt{3}}$

Further

1. Rationalise the denominator of $\frac{3}{7 - \sqrt{5}}$ (2 marks)

2. Show that $\frac{4}{\frac{1}{\sqrt{5}} + 1}$ can be written as $5 - \sqrt{5}$ (3 marks)

3. Expand and simplify $(5 + \sqrt{3})^2 - (5 - \sqrt{3})^2$ (3 marks)

4. $(w - 3\sqrt{5})^2 = z - 72\sqrt{5}$

   Work out the values of w and z.   (3 marks)

5. The diagram shows a right-angled triangle.

   Work out the area of the triangle, giving your answer in the form $a\sqrt{b}$ where a and b are integers.   (4 marks)

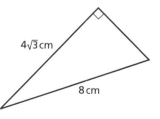

6. The volume of a cylinder is $\sqrt{800}\pi$ cm³

   The height of the cylinder is $\sqrt{2}$ cm.

   Work out the length of the radius of the cylinder.

   Give your answer in the form $a\sqrt{b}$ where a and b are integers.   (3 marks)

7. The first two terms of a geometric sequence are $\sqrt{3} + 1$, 2, ...

   Work out the next two terms in the sequence.   (4 marks)

1.5 Converting between recurring decimals and fractions

White Rose Maths

Foundations

1 Write each decimal as a fraction in its simplest form.

   a) 0.7   **b)** 0.32   **c)** 0.04   **d)** 0.483   **e)** 0.808

2 If $x = 0.27$, write down the value of:

   a) $10x$ **b)** $100x$ **c)** $1000x$

Facts

You can convert any fraction to a decimal by interpreting the fraction as a division and using a written method. When you see that one of the digits in the decimal part of the number is repeating, you know that the decimal will be recurring.

For example, when writing $\frac{4}{9}$ as a decimal, the corresponding division gives:

$$\begin{array}{r} 0 \ . \ 4 \quad 4 \ \dots \\ \hline 9 \, \big|\, 4 \ . \ ^40 \quad ^40 \ \dots \end{array}$$

> The remainder will continue to be 4 and consequently the digit 4 in the decimal will recur.

You would then write 0.44444... as $0.\dot{4}$, which is read 'nought point 4 recurring'.

A dot is placed over the decimal part that recurs. For example:

$0.7222222... = 0.7\dot{2}$

$0.63636363... = 0.\dot{6}\dot{3}$

$0.845845845... = 0.\dot{8}4\dot{5}$

> If more than one digit recurs, place a dot over the first and last digit in the recurring part.

All recurring decimals are **rational** as they can be written in the form $\frac{a}{b}$ where a and b are integers and $b \neq 0$. To convert a recurring decimal to a fraction, you need to use algebra and manipulate the number until the decimal parts are equal, as shown in the examples below.

Focus

Example 1

Write $\frac{5}{6}$ as a decimal.

$\frac{5}{6} = 5 \div 6$	Interpret the fraction as a division.
$$\begin{array}{r} 0 \ . \ 8 \quad 3 \quad 3 \ \dots \\ \hline 6 \, \big|\, 5 \ . \ ^50 \quad ^20 \quad ^20 \ \dots \end{array}$$	Perform the division using the short division method. When one of the digits repeats, you have found the recurring part of the decimal.
$\frac{5}{6} = 0.8\dot{3}$	Use the dot notation for the recurring part.

Example 2

Write $0.3\dot{2}$ as a fraction in its simplest form.

Let $x = 0.322222...$	Call the number x.
$10x = 3.222...$	Multiply both sides of the equation by 10 so that when you subtract you can eliminate the recurring part.
$9x = 2.9$	$10x - x = 9x$
$90x = 29$	Multiply by 10 so there is no decimal part.
$x = \frac{29}{90}$	Solve the resulting equation to find x as a fraction.

Example 3

Write $0.6\dot{3}\dot{2}$ as a fraction in its simplest form.

Let $x = 0.63232323...$	Put the decimal equal to a variable.
$10x = 6.32323232...$ $100x = 63.2323232...$	Multiply the decimal by increasing powers of 10 until the decimal parts are equal.
$1000x = 632.323232...$	The decimal parts are now equal for $1000x$ and $10x$ so you can subtract $10x$ from $1000x$.
$990x = 626$ $x = \frac{626}{990}$	Solve the resulting equation to find x as a fraction.
$= \frac{313}{495}$	Simplify the fraction.

Fluency

1 Circle the fractions that are equivalent to recurring decimals.

$\frac{1}{3}$ $\frac{2}{5}$ $\frac{4}{7}$ $\frac{13}{25}$ $\frac{3}{8}$ $\frac{6}{11}$

2 Write each fraction as a recurring decimal.

a) $\frac{2}{9}$ b) $\frac{4}{9}$ c) $\frac{7}{9}$ d) $\frac{5}{7}$ e) $\frac{6}{11}$ f) $\frac{1}{6}$ g) $\frac{5}{6}$

3 Write each decimal as a fraction.

a) 0.555555...   b) 0.73737373...   c) 0.438438438...

d) 0.066666...   e) 0.375757575...   f) 0.5901901901...

4 Write each decimal as a fraction. Give your answers in their simplest forms.

a) $0.\dot{1}$ b) $0.4\dot{6}$ c) $0.0\dot{3}$ d) $0.08\dot{1}$

e) $0.7\dot{1}$ f) $0.35\dot{2}$ g) $0.\dot{2}8\dot{2}$ h) $0.4\dot{1}5\dot{7}$

5 Express the recurring decimal $4.0\dot{6}$ as a mixed number. Give your answer in its simplest form.

6 Express the recurring decimal $3.\dot{7}\dot{2}$ as a fraction. Give your answer in its simplest form.

7 Express the recurring decimal $1.03\dot{1}$ as a mixed number. Give your answer in its simplest form.

8 Work out $\sqrt{0.\dot{4}}$, giving your answer as a fraction in its simplest form.

Further

1 Work out $0.\dot{4} \times 0.\dot{8}\dot{1}$ as a fraction in its simplest form.   (3 marks)

2 The recurring decimal $0.\dot{3}\dot{6}$ can be written as the fraction $\frac{4}{11}$

Write the decimal $0.4\dot{3}\dot{6}$ as a fraction.   (3 marks)

3 Work out the subtraction. Give your answer as a fraction in its simplest form.

$0.\dot{7} - 0.\dot{2}\dot{3}$ (3 marks)

4 Work out the calculation. Give your answer as a fraction in its simplest form.

$0.1\dot{2} + 0.\dot{3} \div 0.\dot{4}$ (4 marks)

5 Write this list of numbers in ascending order. $0.28\dot{5}$ $\frac{2}{7}$ $\frac{1}{4}$ $\frac{285}{999}$ (3 marks)

6 If $x = 0.\dot{n}$, where n is a digit, determine the value of $0.3\dot{n}$ in terms of x.   (3 marks)

7 If $y = 0.\dot{m}$, where m is a digit, determine the value of $0.5\dot{m}$ in terms of y.   (3 marks)

1.6 Exact answers

Foundations

1. Write the formula for the area of a circle.
2. Write $\sqrt{18}$ in the form $k\sqrt{2}$ where k is an integer.

Facts

An answer that is **exact** is not rounded or approximated in any way.

Decimal answers are not usually exact as they may have been rounded or truncated. If they are exact, it is better to write them in fractional form to show this, for example writing 0.17 as $\frac{17}{100}$

When working with time, it is easier to convert any decimal part of an answer into other units.

For example, 2.57 hours:

= 2 hours and 0.57 × 60 = 34.2 minutes

= 2 hours 34 minutes and 0.2 × 60 = 12 seconds

= 2 hours 34 minutes 12 seconds

Other ways to represent an answer in exact form include multiples of π (pi) or surds.

See unit 1.4 for more details about surds.

Focus

Example 1

Work out the perimeter of the semi-circle.

Give your answer in terms of π

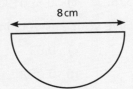

8 cm

Arc length $= \frac{1}{2} \times \pi \times 8 = 4\pi$ cm	Find the arc length of the semi-circle by finding half of the circumference, which is given by $C = \pi d$
Perimeter $= (4\pi + 8)$ cm	Find the total perimeter by adding the arc length and the diameter.

Example 2

Solve $x^2 - 10x + 4 = 0$, giving your solutions in the form $a + \sqrt{b}$ where a and b are integers.

$x^2 - 10x + 4 \equiv (x - 5)^2 - 25 + 4$ $(x - 5)^2 - 21 = 0$	Write the quadratic in 'completed square' form. See unit 2.13 for more details about completing the square.
$(x - 5)^2 = 21$	Add 21 to both sides of the equation.
$x - 5 = \pm\sqrt{21}$	Square root both sides of the equation. Remember that the square root gives a positive and a negative root.
$x = 5 + \sqrt{21}$ or $x = 5 - \sqrt{21}$	Add 5 to both sides to express x in the required form $a + \sqrt{b}$, writing each solution separately.

You could also use the quadratic formula to solve the equation.

Example 3

Find the exact length of AB.

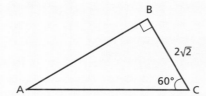

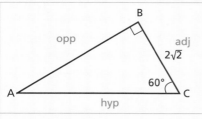

	Labelling the triangle in relation to the angle of 60° indicates that tan(60°) will be involved in calculating AB.
$\tan \theta = \dfrac{\text{opp}}{\text{adj}}$ $\sqrt{3} = \dfrac{AB}{2\sqrt{2}}$	Use the formula for $\tan \theta = \dfrac{\text{opp}}{\text{adj}}$ and $\tan(60°) = \sqrt{3}$ to find the length of AB.
	Exact trigonometric values are given in unit 4F3 and discussed in detail in the *Collins White Rose Maths AQA GCSE 9–1 Revision Guide – Aiming for Grade 5/6.*
$AB = 2\sqrt{6}$	Multiply both sides by $2\sqrt{2}$ to get the answer, using the fact that $\sqrt{a} \times \sqrt{b} = \sqrt{ab}$

Fluency

1 A train travels 338 km at a constant speed of 100 km/h.

Work out the exact amount of time the train travels. Give your answer in hours, minutes and seconds.

2 Find the exact roots of $x^2 - 3x + 1 = 0$

3 The perimeter of a square is 32 cm.

Find the exact length of a diagonal of the square.

4 Find the exact height, h, of the isosceles triangle.

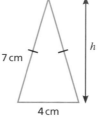

7 cm

4 cm

5 The shape is made using a semi-circle and a quarter-circle.

Find: **a)** the area of the shape   **b)** the perimeter of the shape

Give your answers in terms of π

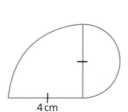

4 cm

Further

1 Work out the fraction of the rectangle that the shaded triangle occupies.   (3 marks)

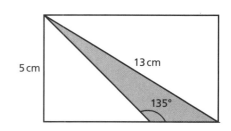

5 cm

13 cm

135°

2 A unit square contains two congruent semi-circles.

The diameter of the semi-circles is equal to the side length of the square.

Express the area of the shaded region in terms of π (3 marks)

Facts

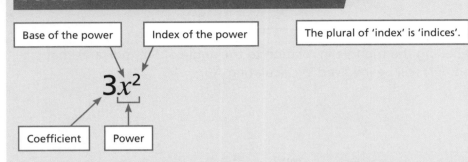

| Base of the power | | Index of the power | | The plural of 'index' is 'indices'. |

$3x^2$

Coefficient | Power

Terms involving indices can only be added or subtracted if they have the same power.

For example, $3x^4 + 2x^3 - x^4 + 11z^3 + 5x^3 \equiv 2x^4 + 7x^3 + 11z^3$

There are three **laws of indices**:

Law	Example 1	Example 2
$x^a \times x^b = x^{a+b}$	$3^2 \times 3^5 = 3^{2+5} = 3^7$	$p^6 \times p^{-2} = p^4$
$x^a \div x^b = x^{a-b}$	$2^7 \div 2^3 = 2^{7-3} = 2^4$	$q^3 \div q^{-2} = q^5$
$(x^a)^b = x^{ab}$	$(5^3)^4 = 5^{3 \times 4} = 5^{12}$	$(2r^3)^5 = 2^5 \times r^{3 \times 5} = 32r^{15}$

For complex expressions, consider each number or letter in turn. For example:

$3a^4b^7 \times 6a^8b = 3 \times 6 \times a^4 \times a^8 \times b^7 \times b = 18a^{12}b^8$

Notice that using the division law, $t^3 \div t^5 = t^{-2}$

An alternative method to divide powers expressed as a fraction is to use cancelling:

$$\frac{t^3}{t^5} = \frac{\cancel{t} \times \cancel{t} \times \cancel{t}}{t \times t \times \cancel{t} \times \cancel{t} \times \cancel{t}} = \frac{1}{t \times t} = \frac{1}{t^2}$$

So you can see that $t^{-2} = \frac{1}{t^2}$

In general, $x^{-a} = \frac{1}{x^a}$ so for example $3^{-2} = \frac{1}{3^2} = \frac{1}{9}$ and $\left(\frac{3}{4}\right)^{-3} = \left(\frac{4}{3}\right)^3 = \frac{64}{27}$

$x^0 = 1$ for any value of x.

Another application of indices is **standard form**, which is a way to write large and small numbers more efficiently in the form $A \times 10^n$, where $1 \leq A < 10$ and n is an integer.

For example, $600\,000 = 6 \times 10^5$ and $0.0047 = 4.7 \times 10^{-3}$

You can use the laws of indices to perform calculations with numbers in standard form.

For example:

$(8 \times 10^5) \times (2 \times 10^{-3}) = (8 \times 2) \times 10^{5+-3} = 16 \times 10^2 = 1.6 \times 10^3$

$(8 \times 10^5) \div (2 \times 10^{-3}) = (8 \div 2) \times 10^{5--3} = 4 \times 10^8$

$(4 \times 10^5)^3 = 4^3 \times 10^{5 \times 3} = 64 \times 10^{15} = 6.4 \times 10^{16}$

On your calculator, enter standard form numbers using the ×10ˣ or EXP buttons and use the operation keys as usual. Check that you get the same answers as given above.

Practice

1 Simplify:

a) $a^3 + 7a^3$

b) $4(9b^5)$

c) $2c^9 - 2c^8 + 8c^9 + 4c^8$

2 Simplify:

a) $d^{10} \times d^6$

b) $f^4 \times 2f^3$

c) $g^{17} \times g^6 \times g^{27}$

d) $2h^5 \times 5h^2$

e) $3z^7y^2 \times 6yz$

f) $-8x^2n^{-4} \times -4x^{-1}n^7$

g) $3t^{4.4} \times -5t^{2.6} \times t^{-2}$

h) $0.3f^{0.4} \times 100f^{1.6}$

3 Simplify:

a) $j^8 \div j^2$

b) $21k^{10} \div 3k^5$

c) $\dfrac{m^{16}n^{12}}{n^{11}m^4}$

d) $\dfrac{30p^{13}q^7}{6p^{13}q^{-4}}$

e) $15r^{-2} \div 24r^{-8}$

f) $\dfrac{5d^3 \times 12d^7}{20d^{10}}$

g) $\dfrac{8y^{11} \times 7x^4y}{7y^{13} \times 2x^3}$

h) $\dfrac{45a^3 \times 4b^{-9}}{8a^{-15} \times 9b^{-4}}$

4 Simplify:

a) $(q^5)^3$

b) $(r^{0.2})^{0.3}$

c) $\left(h^{\frac{1}{3}}\right)^{\frac{3}{4}}$

d) $(3f^3)^3$

5 Work out:

a) $4^{14} \div 4^{11}$

b) 15^0

c) 3^{-2}

d) $10^{-2} \times 3^4$

6 Simplify:

a) $\dfrac{(a^{12})^3}{(a^4)^8}$

b) $\dfrac{30m^8n^{-1}}{12m^{-2}n^{-2}}$

7 $64^2 = 4^c$

Which is the correct value of c?

1.5   5   6   32

8 Work out w if $r^3 \times r^2 = r^5 \times r^w$

9 Simplify $\dfrac{g^{\frac{2}{3}} \times g^{\frac{1}{5}}}{g^{\frac{1}{4}}}$

10 Solve $4^{3x+2} = 4^{11} \times 4^3$

11 Find the value of k such that: $(k \times \sqrt[3]{125})^{-2} = \dfrac{1}{225}$

12 Write these numbers in standard form.

a) 137 000

b) 13 700 000

c) 0.000 137

13 Convert these numbers into ordinary form.

a) 4.57×10^4

b) 4.57×10^{-2}

c) 4.0507×10^3

14 Calculate:

a) $(4.57 \times 10^4) + (1.22 \times 10^3)$

b) $(4.57 \times 10^4) - (1.22 \times 10^3)$

15 Calculate:

a) $(3.2 \times 10^{-2}) \times (2 \times 10^7)$

b) $(4.5 \times 10^3) \div (9 \times 10^4)$

Facts

Equations can be solved using **inverse operations** and 'balancing' both sides.

$$-22 \left(\begin{array}{c} 5a + 22 = 15 \\ 5a = -7 \\ a = -1.4 \end{array} \right) \begin{array}{c} -22 \\ \div 5 \end{array}$$
$$\div 5$$

$$-1 \left(\begin{array}{c} \frac{b}{3} + 1 = 60 \\ \frac{b}{3} = 59 \\ b = 177 \end{array} \right) \begin{array}{c} -1 \\ \times 3 \end{array}$$

You can also use bar models to illustrate solving equations.

| t | t | t | t | t | t | t | 14 |
| t | t | 22 |

| t | t | t | t | t | 14 |
| 22 |

| t | t | t | t | t |
| 8 |

| t | t | t | t | t |
| 1.6 | 1.6 | 1.6 | 1.6 | 1.6 |

$$-2t \left(\begin{array}{c} 14 + 7t = 2t + 22 \\ 14 + 5t = 22 \end{array} \right) -2t$$
$$-14 \left(\begin{array}{c} 14 + 5t = 22 \\ 5t = 8 \end{array} \right) -14$$
$$\div 5 \left(\begin{array}{c} 5t = 8 \\ t = 1.6 \end{array} \right) \div 5$$

Inequalities can be approached in the same way.

$$+14 \left(\begin{array}{c} 13 > 3y - 14 \\ 27 > 3y \\ 9 > y \end{array} \right) \begin{array}{c} +14 \\ \div 3 \end{array}$$

$$-12 \left(\begin{array}{c} 6 \leq \frac{k}{8} + 12 \\ -6 \leq \frac{k}{8} \\ -48 \leq k \end{array} \right) \begin{array}{c} -12 \\ \times 8 \end{array}$$

Remember that if you multiply or divide both sides of an inequality by a negative number, the direction of the inequality is reversed.

$$\div -7 \left(\begin{array}{c} -7t > -14 \\ t < 2 \end{array} \right) \div -7$$

Generally, if the unknown in an equation or an inequality has a negative coefficient, deal with this term first to make it easier to solve.

$$+4r \left(\begin{array}{c} 5 = 20 - 4r \\ 5 + 4r = 20 \end{array} \right) +4r$$

Then solve as normal

$$+\frac{d}{9} \left(\begin{array}{c} -3 \leq -\frac{d}{9} + 12 \\ \frac{d}{9} - 3 \leq 12 \end{array} \right) +\frac{d}{9}$$

Then solve as normal

You can solve equations with brackets by expanding the brackets first or by division.

$$+48 \left(\begin{array}{c} 12(x - 4) = 42 \\ 12x - 48 = 42 \\ 12x = 90 \\ x = 7.5 \end{array} \right) \begin{array}{c} +48 \\ \div 12 \end{array}$$

OR

$$\div 12 \left(\begin{array}{c} 12(x - 4) = 42 \\ x - 4 = 3.5 \\ x = 7.5 \end{array} \right) \begin{array}{c} \div 12 \\ +4 \end{array}$$

The **subject** of a formula is the variable being worked out in the formula. For example, in $F = ma$, F is the subject. You can **rearrange a formula** to make a different variable the subject by using inverse operations (in the same way as when solving equations).

Making a the subject of $F = ma$

$$\div m \left(\begin{array}{c} \frac{F}{m} = a \end{array} \right) \div m$$

Making I the subject of $V = \frac{I}{R}$

$$\times R \left(\begin{array}{c} VR = I \end{array} \right) \times R$$

Rearranging some formulae can involve multiple steps.

Rearranging $a = \dfrac{c + bm}{d}$ to make m the subject

Making b the subject of $a = \sqrt{b^2 - c}$

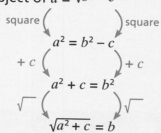

$\times d \left(\right) \times d$

$ad = c + bm$

$-c \left(\right) -c$

$ad - c = bm$

$\div b \left(\right) \div b$

$\dfrac{ad - c}{b} = m$

square $\left(\right)$ square

$a^2 = b^2 - c$

$+c \left(\right) +c$

$a^2 + c = b^2$

$\sqrt{} \left(\right) \sqrt{}$

$\sqrt{a^2 + c} = b$

Practice

1. Solve the equations.

   a) $2x + 5 = 30$ b) $2x - 5 = 30$ c) $2(x + 5) = 30$ d) $2(x - 5) = 30$

   e) $\dfrac{x}{2} + 5 = 30$ f) $\dfrac{x + 2}{5} = 30$ g) $\dfrac{x - 2}{5} = 30$ h) $\dfrac{x}{2} - 5 = 30$

2. Solve the inequalities.

   a) $2x + 5 > 30$ b) $2x - 5 < 30$ c) $2(x + 5) \geqslant 30$ d) $2(x - 5) < 30$

   e) $\dfrac{x}{2} + 5 \geqslant 30$ f) $\dfrac{x + 2}{5} < 30$ g) $\dfrac{x - 2}{5} \geqslant 30$ h) $\dfrac{x}{2} - 5 < 30$

3. Darius thinks of a number.

   6 more than one-quarter of Darius's number is 11

   Work out Darius's number.

4. Samira thinks of a number.

   7 less than triple Samira's number is less than 30

   Work out the greatest possible integer value that Samira's number could be.

5. Solve the equations.

   a) $15 + 2t = t + 21$ b) $15 - 2u = u + 21$ c) $15 - 2v = 21 - v$

6. Solve the equations.

   a) $10 + 8a = 20$ b) $10 - 8a = 20$

7. Solve the inequalities.

   a) $3 + \dfrac{y}{10} \leqslant 5$ b) $3 - \dfrac{y}{10} \leqslant 5$

8. Solve $72 = 6(5p - 3)$

9. $1 - 5x \geqslant -16$

   Work out the greatest integer value of x.

10. Make x the subject of:

    a) $z = \dfrac{x - w}{y}$ b) $k = a + \dfrac{x}{c}$ c) $d = \dfrac{f - x}{h}$ d) $m = vx^2 - t$

11. Rearrange $t = \sqrt{\dfrac{V}{K^2}}$ to express K in terms of V and t.

    'Express K in terms of V and t' is another way of saying 'Make K the subject of the formula'.

12. A right-angled triangle has base a cm and perpendicular height b cm.

    The area of the triangle is K cm^2

    Express b in terms of a and K.

2.1 Changing the subject with unknowns on both sides

Foundations

1 Rearrange the formulae to make x the subject.

a) $y = x(r + 3)$ b) $h = 2w + 5x$ c) $5b - 4 = x(3 - 2m)$

2 Factorise:

a) $5x + bx$ b) $wh + jw$ c) $ay - y$

Facts

A **formula** is a rule connecting variables written with mathematical symbols. The plural of formula is **formulae**. The **subject** of a formula is the variable that is expressed in terms of other variables. For example, x is the subject of the formula $x = 5y + 3p$. You could also say that x is expressed **in terms of** y and p.

You can **change the subject of** or rearrange a formula using inverse operations in the same way you would solve an equation. Changing the subject of simple formulae is covered in unit 2F2. In more complex formulae, the same variable can appear more than once and you may need to factorise, expand brackets, or both, as steps in the rearrangement.

Focus

Example 1

Make a the subject of the formulae.

a) $C = 2a + ba$ b) $h(b + a) = k(f - a)$

a)
$$C = 2a + ba$$

Factorise

$$C = a(2 + b)$$

$\div (2 + b)$ $\left(\dfrac{C}{2 + b} = a\right)$ $\div (2 + b)$

$$a = \frac{C}{2 + b}$$

To make a the subject you need to isolate a.

Here you need to factorise.

You now need to divide both sides of the formula by $(2 + b)$.

You don't have to show the brackets around the 2 and b in the denominator.

| It is usual to write the formula with the subject first. |

b)
Expand $\left($ $h(b + a) = k(f - a)$ $\right)$ Expand

$+ ka$ $\left($ $hb + ha = kf - ka$ $\right)$ $+ ka$

$- hb$ $\left($ $hb + ha + ka = kf$ $\right)$ $- hb$

$$ha + ka = kf - hb$$

Factorise $\left($ $a(h + k) = kf - hb$ $\right)$

$\div (h + k)$ $\left($ $a = \dfrac{kf - hb}{h + k}$ $\right)$ $\div (h + k)$

Start by expanding the brackets to get all the terms in a.

You need to get all the terms that contain a to one side of the formula. You can do this by adding ka and subtracting hb from both sides.

Now that you have just a terms on the left-hand side, you can isolate a by factorising.

Finally, divide both sides of the formula by $(h + k)$ to make a the subject.

Example 2

Rearrange $x = \dfrac{y + 1}{w - y}$ to make y the subject of the formula.

$\times (w - y)$	$x = \dfrac{y + 1}{w - y}$	$\times (w - y)$
Expand	$x(w - y) = y + 1$	
$+ xy$	$xw - xy = y + 1$	$+ xy$
$- 1$	$xw = y + 1 + xy$	$- 1$
	$xw - 1 = y + xy$	Factorise
$\div (1 + x)$	$xw - 1 = y(1 + x)$	$\div (1 + x)$
	$\dfrac{xw - 1}{1 + x} = y$	
	$y = \dfrac{xw - 1}{1 + x}$	

Multiply by $(w - y)$ to clear the fraction as this will help you get the terms in y together.

Before you can isolate y, you need to use inverse operations to get all the y terms to one side of the formula.

Then you can factorise.

Finally, divide by $(1 + x)$ to make y the subject.

Fluency

1 Make h the subject of each formula.

a) $y = 5h + 3h$ b) $y = 5h - 3h$ c) $y = 5h + rh$ d) $y = wh - rh$

2 The surface area of a cuboid is given by the formula $A = 2lw + 2lh + 2hw$

Find a formula for l in terms of A, h and w.

3 Rearrange $7bc - 7d = de + 2bc$ to make:

a) b the subject   b) c the subject   c) d the subject

4 Make y the subject of each formula.

a) $4(y + x) = 9(y - w)$

b) $4(y + x) = b(y - w)$

c) $a(y + x) = b(w - y)$

5 Rearrange each formula to make w the subject.

a) $D = \dfrac{p + w}{w}$ b) $D = \dfrac{w}{p + w}$

6 Rearrange the formulae to express k in terms of m.

a) $m = \dfrac{k + 5}{k + 7}$ b) $m = \dfrac{k + 5}{k - 7}$ c) $m = \dfrac{k + 5}{7 - k}$ d) $m = \dfrac{5 - k}{7 - k}$

Further

1 Rearrange the formula $\dfrac{1}{x} + \dfrac{1}{y} = \dfrac{1}{z}$ to make y the subject.   (3 marks)

2 Make p the subject of each formula.

a) $\dfrac{pa - b}{t - a} = a + p$ (3 marks)

b) $\dfrac{p - t}{a - p} = \dfrac{t}{a}$ (3 marks)

c) $\sqrt{\dfrac{p - a}{p + t}} = \dfrac{a}{4t}$ (4 marks)

2.2 Algebraic fractions

White Rose Maths

Foundations

1 Work out:
    a) $\frac{2}{3} - \frac{1}{5}$ b) $\frac{7}{8} \times \frac{4}{5}$ c) $\frac{3}{5} \div \frac{9}{10}$

2 Factorise:
    a) $6y + 24$ b) $y^2 + y$ c) $x^2 - 2x - 24$ d) $x^2 - 1$

Facts

An **algebraic fraction** is a fraction whose numerator and/or denominator are algebraic expressions.

You can **add** or **subtract** algebraic fractions in the same way as numerical fractions, by converting them to equivalent fractions with a common denominator and then adding or subtracting the numerators.

You can **cancel** common **factors** in algebraic fractions. It is sometimes useful to do this before **multiplying** or **dividing** algebraic expressions.

Focus

Example 1

Write each of these as a single algebraic fraction. Give your answer in its simplest form.

a) $\frac{4x - 1}{5} + \frac{x + 2}{3}$ b) $\frac{5}{4x - 1} - \frac{3}{x + 2}$

a) $\frac{4x - 1}{5} + \frac{x + 2}{3} = \frac{3(4x - 1)}{15} + \frac{5(x + 2)}{15}$	Start by rewriting both fractions with a common denominator.
$= \frac{12x - 3}{15} + \frac{5x + 10}{15}$	Expand the brackets in the numerators.
$= \frac{12x - 3 + 5x + 10}{15} = \frac{17x + 7}{15}$	Write as a single fraction then simplify the expression in the numerator by adding like terms.
b) $\frac{5}{4x - 1} - \frac{3}{x + 2} = \frac{5(x + 2)}{(4x - 1)(x + 2)} - \frac{3(4x - 1)}{(4x - 1)(x + 2)}$	Start by rewriting both fractions with a common denominator. You don't need to expand the binomials in the denominator.
$= \frac{5x + 10}{(4x - 1)(x + 2)} - \frac{12x - 3}{(4x - 1)(x + 2)}$	Expand the brackets in the numerators so that you can simplify.
$= \frac{5x + 10 - 12x + 3}{(4x - 1)(x + 2)}$	Now write as a single fraction. Be careful of the negative term. $5x + 10 - (12x - 3) = 5x + 10 - 12x + 3$
$= \frac{13 - 7x}{(4x - 1)(x + 2)}$	Simplify the numerator.

Example 2

Write each expression as a fraction in its simplest form.

a) $\frac{3y - 2}{10y} \div \frac{12y - 8}{5y^2}$ b) $\frac{x^2 + x - 12}{5x - 15}$

a) $\frac{3y - 2}{10y} \div \frac{12y - 8}{5y^2} = \frac{3y - 2}{10y} \times \frac{5y^2}{12y - 8}$	To divide a fraction, you multiply by its reciprocal.
$\frac{3y - 2}{10y} \times \frac{5y^2}{4(3y - 2)}$	$12y - 8$ can be factorised to give $4(3y - 2)$
$\frac{\cancel{3y - 2}}{_2\cancel{10y}} \times \frac{\cancel{5}y^{\cancel{2}}}{4(\cancel{3y - 2})}$	Cancel the common factors before multiplying. In this case, you can cancel the common factor $3y - 2$ You can also cancel the common factors 5 and y.
$\frac{1}{2} \times \frac{y}{4} = \frac{y}{8}$	You can now multiply the fractions.

b) $\dfrac{x^2 + x - 12}{5x - 15} = \dfrac{(x - 3)(x + 4)}{5(x - 3)}$	Factorise first.
$\dfrac{(x-3)(x + 4)}{5(x-3)} = \dfrac{x + 4}{5}$	You can cancel the common factor $x - 3$

Fluency

1 Write each expression as a single fraction in its simplest form.

a) $\dfrac{2p}{3} - \dfrac{p}{5}$

b) $\dfrac{p + 2}{3} + \dfrac{p}{5}$

c) $\dfrac{p + 2}{3} + \dfrac{p - 3}{5}$

d) $\dfrac{p + 2}{3} - \dfrac{p - 3}{5}$

2 Simplify:

a) $\dfrac{m^2}{4} \times \dfrac{2}{m}$

b) $\dfrac{3m}{4} \div \dfrac{m}{12}$

c) $\dfrac{6m^2}{7t} \times \dfrac{21t}{8}$

d) $\dfrac{10m^3}{12} \div \dfrac{5m}{4}$

3 Write the answer to each calculation as a single fraction.

a) $\dfrac{3}{x + 1} + \dfrac{2}{x + 3}$

b) $\dfrac{3}{x - 1} + \dfrac{2}{x + 3}$

c) $\dfrac{3}{x + 1} - \dfrac{2}{x - 3}$

d) $\dfrac{3}{x - 1} - \dfrac{2}{x - 3}$

4 Write each of these as a single algebraic fraction. Give your answer in its simplest form.

a) $\dfrac{h + 8}{5} \times \dfrac{3h}{4}$

b) $\dfrac{h + 8}{5} \div \dfrac{3h}{4}$

c) $\dfrac{h + 8}{5} \times \dfrac{4}{3h}$

d) $\dfrac{h + 8}{5} \div \dfrac{4}{3h}$

5 Express as a single fraction in its simplest form:

a) $\dfrac{3k - 2}{3} + \dfrac{4k + 1}{2}$

b) $\dfrac{3k - 2}{3} - \dfrac{4k + 1}{2}$

c) $\dfrac{3}{3k - 2} + \dfrac{2}{4k + 1}$

d) $\dfrac{3}{3k - 2} - \dfrac{2}{4k + 1}$

6 Write each expression in its simplest form.

a) $\dfrac{f + 5}{6} \times \dfrac{f + 3}{3}$

b) $\dfrac{f + 5}{f} \div \dfrac{f + 3}{f}$

c) $\dfrac{6}{f - 5} \times \dfrac{f - 5}{3}$

d) $\dfrac{6}{f - 5} \div \dfrac{f + 3}{3}$

7 Write each expression in its simplest form.

a) $\dfrac{x + 3}{4} \times \dfrac{7}{2x + 6}$

b) $\dfrac{2x - 5}{8} \div \dfrac{6x - 15}{2}$

c) $\dfrac{4x - 7}{9} \times \dfrac{6}{12x - 21}$

d) $\dfrac{15}{x - 1} \div \dfrac{3}{x^2 - x}$

e) $\dfrac{x^2 + 9x + 20}{x^2 + 3x - 4}$

f) $\dfrac{x^2 - 5x + 6}{x^2 - 9}$

Further

1 Write the calculations as single fractions in their simplest form.

a) $\dfrac{2x + 6}{x^2 + 8x + 15} \times \dfrac{x^2 + 11x + 28}{x + 4}$ (3 marks)

b) $3x + 15 \times \dfrac{x^2 - 2x + 1}{(x + 5)(x^2 + 4x - 5)}$ (3 marks)

c) $\dfrac{x^2 + 10x + 24}{x^2 - 3x - 28} \div \dfrac{x^2 + 2x - 24}{x^2 - 16}$ (3 marks)

2 Write $\dfrac{2x^2 + 5x - 12}{x^2 + x - 12}$ in the form $\dfrac{ax + b}{x + c}$ where a, b and c are integers. (3 marks)

3 Work out, in terms of y, the mean of these three expressions. (3 marks)

$\dfrac{y + 3}{15}$ $\dfrac{y + 1}{5}$ $\dfrac{y}{3}$

4 A linear sequence has first term $\dfrac{2}{x + 3}$ and second term $\dfrac{3}{x + 4}$

Work out the next term in the sequence. (4 marks)

2.3 Expanding and factorising

Foundations

1 Expand and simplify:

  a) $4(x + 1) + 2(3x - 3)$ **b)** $8(3y - 3) - 4(5 - 2y)$

2 Factorise:

  a) $6x^2 - 8x$ **b)** $6x^2 - 8x + 4xy$ **c)** $x^2 + 5x + 6$ **d)** $x^2 + 5x - 6$

Facts

You **expand** by multiplying to remove brackets. You may then need to **simplify** the expression by collecting like terms.

A **binomial** is an expression involving the sum or difference of two terms, like $a + 3$ or $2b - 5$. When expanding binomials, you need to multiply each term in the first bracket by each term in the second bracket. Algebra tiles are a useful way of representing this process.

You **factorise** an expression by finding the factors that you need to multiply together to make the expression.

You **simplify** an expression by rewriting it in a simpler form.

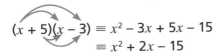

$$(x + 5)(x - 3) \equiv x^2 - 3x + 5x - 15$$
$$\equiv x^2 + 2x - 15$$

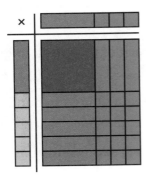

Focus

Example 1
Expand and simplify $(2p - 1)(3p - 4)$

	Multiply each term in the first bracket by each term in the second bracket, taking care with the coefficients and the signs:
$(2p - 1)(3p - 4) \equiv 6p^2 - 8p - 3p + 4$	$2p \times 3p = 6p^2$, $2p \times -4 = -8p$, $-1 \times 3p = -3p$ and $-1 \times -4 = 4$
$\equiv 6p^2 - 11p + 4$	Then simplify by collecting like terms.

Example 2
Factorise: a) $2x^2 + 7x - 15$ b) $64x^2 - 25$

a) $2x^2 + 7x - 15 \equiv$ $2x^2$ $(2x \quad)(x \quad)$	The factors of 2 are 1 and 2 so you know one bracket must contain a $2x$ term and the other bracket must contain an x (which is the same as $1x$) term.
Factor pairs of -15: 1 -15 -1 15 3 -5 -3 5	List the factor pairs of -15 It is useful to list them as pairs so that you are less likely to miss any out.
$10x$ $(2x - 3)(x + 5)$ $-3x$	Now try the different factor pairs in the brackets. Remember, the sum of the x terms needs to be $7x$. $10x - 3x = 7x$, so the only possible solution is as shown.
$2x^2 + 7x - 15 \equiv (2x - 3)(x + 5)$	You can check your solution by expanding $(2x - 3)(x + 5)$

b) $64x^2 - 25 = 64x^2 + 0x - 25$	It may help to rewrite the expression like this.
$+40x$ $(8x - 5)(8x + 5)$ $-40x$	You need the product of the first two terms in the brackets to be $64x^2$ and the product of the last two terms to be -25. When you find the sum of the x terms, you want them to equal zero. Both 64 and 25 are square numbers. x^2 is also a square, so $64x^2$ is a square. To factorise this expression, you need to square root each of the terms: $\sqrt{64x^2} = 8x$ and $\sqrt{25} = 5$
$64x^2 - 25 = (8x - 5)(8x + 5)$	Expressions like $64x^2 - 25$ are known as the 'difference of two squares'.

Fluency

1 Expand and simplify:

   a) $(h + 3)(h + 1)$ b) $(g + 5)(g - 2)$ c) $(k - 8)(k + 3)$ d) $(m - 5)(m - 7)$

2 Factorise:

   a) $3x^2 + 7x + 2$ b) $2x^2 + 13x + 15$ c) $5x^2 + 19x + 12$ d) $4x^2 + 16x + 7$

3 Expand and simplify:

   a) $(3t + 5)(t - 1)$ b) $(2u - 3)(3u - 2)$ c) $(2p + 6)(p - 3)$ d) $(2h + 8)(3 - h)$

4 Expand and simplify:

   a) $(2x + 3)(2x - 3)$ b) $(5 - k)(5 + k)$ c) $(6u + 11)(6u - 11)$

   d) $(x + 4)^2$ e) $(y - 6)^2$ f) $(7h - 9)^2$

> In parts c) and d), look for a numerical common factor first.

5 Factorise:

   a) $2x^2 + 5x - 18$ b) $3b^2 - b - 24$ c) $6y^2 + 2y - 8$ d) $2x^2 - 18$

   e) $9x^2 - 81$ f) $144y^2 - 169a^2$ g) $\frac{4}{25}n^2 - \frac{81}{100}$ h) $64a^2 - \frac{1}{4}b^2$

6 Expand and simplify:

   a) $(y + a)(y + b)$ b) $(y + b)(y - b)$ c) $(y - a)(y - b)$

   d) $(a - y)(y + b)$ e) $(y + a)^2$ f) $(y - b)^2$

Further

1 Write expressions for the areas of these shapes.

a)  $(3t - 2)$ m, $(t + 1)$ m   (2 marks)

b) $(u - 5)$ cm   (2 marks)

2 Factorise these expressions.

   a) $3x - 2x^2 + 20$ (2 marks)   b) $3x^2y - 6xy + x - 2$ (2 marks)

   c) $22x - 24 - 4x^2$ (2 marks)   d) $xy + 2y - 3x^2y$ (2 marks)

> If a quadratic expression has a negative x^2 term, you can factorise it by first taking out a factor of -1

3 Work out all the pairs of values for g and h if $(x + g)(3x + h)$ is equivalent to $3x^2 - 48$ (3 marks)

4 The area of a square is $9x^2 - 48x + 64$

Work out an expression for the perimeter of the square.   (3 marks)

2.4 Algebraic proof

Foundations

1 a) Simplify $(9n^2 + 6n + 1) - (9n^2 - 6n + 1)$ b) Expand and simplify $(2n - 1)^2$

2 Factorise: a) $4n^2 + 4n + 2$ b) $(n + 2)(n + 1) + (n + 2)$

Facts

To **prove** something is to show that it is always true. It is not enough to demonstrate with a few numbers; you need to use algebra.

Numbers are **consecutive** if they follow on from each other. For example, 8, 9, 10 are consecutive numbers, and algebraically you could have n, $n + 1$, $n + 2$

Given that n is an integer, then $2n$ must be an **even number** as it is a multiple of 2. In the same way, an **odd number** can be represented by the expression **$2n + 1$**

Even
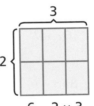
$6 = 2 \times 3$

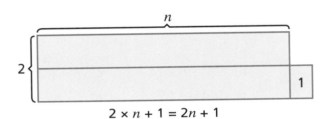
$2 \times n = 2n$

Odd
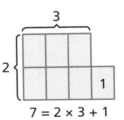
$7 = 2 \times 3 + 1$

$2 \times n + 1 = 2n + 1$

It is also useful to know that $3n$ is a multiple of 3, $4n$ is a multiple of 4, etc.

An **identity** is true for all values of the variables. The sign $\equiv$ means identically equal to.

Focus

Example 1
Prove algebraically that the sum of three consecutive integers is a multiple of 3

Let n be an integer. Three consecutive numbers can be given as n, $n + 1$, $n + 2$	
$n + n + 1 + n + 2 \equiv 3n + 3$	To find the sum, you need to add the three numbers.
$\equiv 3(n + 1)$	To show that the expression is a multiple of 3, you need to factorise to the form '3 multiplied by a number'.
3 is a factor of the total, so the total is a multiple of 3	State your conclusion clearly.

Example 2

Prove that $(2n + 1)^2 - (2n - 1)^2$ is always a multiple of 8, for all positive integer values of n.

$(2n + 1)^2 - (2n - 1)^2$ $\equiv (2n + 1)(2n + 1) - (2n - 1)(2n - 1)$	Start by expanding both pairs of binomials.
$\equiv 4n^2 + 4n + 1 - (4n^2 - 4n + 1)$ $\equiv 4n + 4n$	Simplify by collecting like terms. Be careful with the negative terms. $-(-4n) = +4n$
$\equiv 8n$, which is always a multiple of 8	8 multiplied by a number is always a multiple of 8

Example 3

Prove that the difference between the squares of any two consecutive integers is equal to the sum of the two integers.

Let two consecutive numbers be n and $n + 1$ where n is an integer.	
$(n + 1)^2 - (n)^2 \equiv n^2 + 2n + 1 - n^2$	You need to square each expression and then subtract one from the other.
$\equiv 2n + 1$	Simplify the expression.
$\equiv n + (n + 1)$	Write the expression in the desired form. In this case, you need to show that it is equivalent to the sum of the original expressions used.

Fluency

1. Given that n is an integer, decide if the expressions represent odd or even numbers, or if you cannot tell.

   a) $2n$ b) $2n + 1$ c) $3n$ d) $6n$

   e) $5n$ f) $5(n + 1)$ g) n^2 h) $(2n)^2$

2. An even number can be written in the form $2n$ where n is an integer.

   a) Prove that the square of an even number is always divisible by 4

   b) Write an expression for an odd number.

   c) Prove that the square of an odd number cannot be even.

3. Prove algebraically that the product of any two odd numbers is odd.

4. Prove that $(3n + 1)^2 - (3n - 1)^2$ is always a multiple of 12, for all positive integer values of n.

5. Prove algebraically that the sum of the squares of two consecutive even integers is always a multiple of 4

6. Given that n is an integer, prove algebraically that the sum of $(n + 4)(n + 3)$ and $(n + 4)$ is always a square number.

Further

1. Prove that the sum of any two consecutive integers is equal to the difference between the squares of these integers. (3 marks)

2. Prove algebraically that the sum of the squares of any two even positive integers is always a multiple of 4 (3 marks)

   > You will need to use two different letters to represent the numbers.

3. Prove algebraically that the difference between the squares of any two odd positive integers is always a multiple of 2 (3 marks)

4. Prove that the sum of the squares of two consecutive odd numbers is always 2 greater than a multiple of 8 (3 marks)

5. Prove that the sum of the squares of any three consecutive odd numbers is equal to 1 less than a multiple of 12 (3 marks)

2.5 Functions

Foundations

1 Given that $x = 4$ and $y = -3$, work out:

   a) $4x$ b) $5y$ c) $3x + y$ d) xy^2 e) $x(y + 4)$

2 Solve the equations.

   a) $3x + 1 = 13$ b) $5x - 3 = 18$ c) $\dfrac{3x + 13}{4} = 22$ d) $\dfrac{1}{2}(x + 3) = 19$

Facts

A **function** describes a relationship between a set of input values and a set of output values. This can be shown as a function machine.

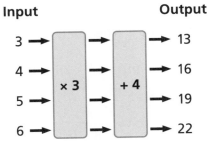

Here, the function is to 'multiply by 3 then add 4'.

For an input x, the output could be written as $3x + 4$

This is usually written as $f(x) = 3x + 4$ | This is read as 'f of x is equal to $3x + 4$'.

The **inverse** of a function $f(x)$, written $f^{-1}(x)$, finds the input for a given output. In the example above, to find the input you would subtract 4 from the output and then divide by 3.

So $f^{-1}(x) = \dfrac{x - 4}{3}$

Composite functions are made when two functions are applied consecutively to the input so that the output from the first function becomes the input to the second. For two functions $f(x)$ and $g(x)$, $fg(x)$ means you apply g first and then f, and $gf(x)$ means you apply f first and then g. See Example 2.

Focus

Example 1

$f(x) = \dfrac{3x + 2}{4}$

a) Work out the value of $f(4)$ b) Find $f^{-1}(x)$

a) $f(4) = \dfrac{3 \times 4 + 2}{4} = \dfrac{14}{4} = \dfrac{7}{2}$	Substitute $x = 4$ in the expression for $f(x)$.
b) $\quad y = \dfrac{3x + 2}{4}$ $\overset{\times 4}{} \qquad \overset{\times 4}{}$ $4y = 3x + 2$ $\overset{-2}{} \qquad \overset{-2}{}$ $4y - 2 = 3x$ $\overset{\div 3}{} \qquad \overset{\div 3}{}$ $\dfrac{4y - 2}{3} = x$	To find the inverse function, form an equation by labelling the output with another letter, such as y. Then rearrange to make x the subject.
$f^{-1}(x) = \dfrac{4x - 2}{3}$	Then rewrite the expression using inverse function notation and the letter x in place of y.

Example 2

$f(x) = 2x + 1$ and $g(x) = 4x - 2$

a) Work out $fg(1)$ b) Work out $ff(3)$ c) Write an expression for $gf(x)$

a) $g(1) = 4 \times 1 - 2 = 2$	$fg(1)$ means you need to work out $g(1)$ first.
$f(2) = 2 \times 2 + 1 = 5$	$g(1) = 2$, so now you need to work out $f(g(1))$, which is the same as $f(2)$. $\boxed{= 2}$
So, $fg(1) = 5$	
b) $f(3) = 2 \times 3 + 1 = 7$	$ff(3)$ means you need to work out $f(3)$ first.
$f(7) = 2 \times 7 + 1 = 15$	$f(3) = 7$, so now you need to work out $f(f(3))$, which is the same as $f(7)$. $\boxed{= 7}$
So, $ff(3) = 15$	
c) $f(x) = 2x + 1$	You need to find an algebraic expression for $gf(x)$. This means you are applying the function f first and then substituting the result into $g(x)$.
$g(f(x)) = 4(f(x)) - 2$	You replace x in $g(x)$ with $f(x)$, i.e. $f(x)$ is the input.
$g(f(x)) = 4(2x + 1) - 2$ $= 8x + 4 - 2$ $= 8x + 2$	Replace $f(x)$ with $2x + 1$ Simplify the expression.

Fluency

1 Find the inverse of each function.

a) $f(x) = 2x + 2$ b) $g(x) = \dfrac{x - 3}{4}$ c) $h(x) = x^2 - 3$

2 $g(x) = 2x^2 + 8$

a) Work out $g(2)$ b) Work out $g(5)$ c) Solve $g(x) = 40$

3 Given $f(x) = \dfrac{3x - 4}{5}$

a) Work out $f(2)$ b) Solve $f^{-1}(x) = 12$

4 Given $f(x) = 3x + 1$ and $g(x) = 9x$

a) Work out $fg(3)$ b) Work out $gg(2)$

5 Given $f(x) = x^2 - 4$ and $g(x) = \dfrac{x}{3}$

a) Work out $f(-3)$ b) Work out $g(12)$ c) Work out $gf(2)$

Further

1 Given $f(x) = 2x + 1$ and $g(x) = x^2$

a) Work out $fg(3)$ (2 marks)

b) Write an expression for $gf(x)$ (2 marks)

2 Given $f(x) = x^2$ and $g(x) = 5x - 6$

Work out values of x such that $f(x) = g(x)$ (3 marks)

3 Given $f(x) = 5x + 6$ and $g(x) = 2x$, solve the equation $fg(x) = 50$ (3 marks)

4 Given $h(x) = x^2 + 1$, find an expression for $h(x + 2)$ (2 marks)

5 Given $f(x) = x^2 + 3$, show that $f(x + 1) + f(x) = 2x^2 + 2x + 7$ (3 marks)

2.6 Parallel and perpendicular lines

White Rose Maths

Foundations

For each equation, state the gradient and the coordinates of the y-intercept.

a) $y = 2x + 4$ b) $y = 5 - 3x$ c) $2y = 6x + 10$ d) $2x + 4y = 10$ e) $3x + 2y + 6 = 0$

Facts

Parallel lines have the same gradient.

$y = 2x + 3$, $y = 2x - 5$, $2y - 8 = 4x$ are all parallel.

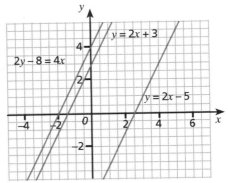

> If you rearrange the equation into the form $y = mx + c$, then m is the gradient of the line.

Two lines are **perpendicular** if they meet at a right angle.

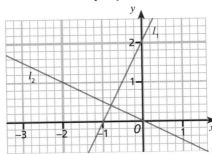

The gradient of line l_1 is 2 and the gradient of line l_2 is $-\frac{1}{2}$

The product of the gradient of two perpendicular lines is -1. In the example above, $2 \times -\frac{1}{2} = -1$

Focus

Example 1

Line l has equation $y = 5x + 2$

a) Work out the equation of a line parallel to l that goes through the point $(0, -2)$
b) Work out the equation of a line perpendicular to l that goes through the point $(0, 7)$

a) $y = 5x + 2$ has a gradient of 5	Lines which are parallel have the same gradient, so the line you need will also have a gradient of 5
Equation is $y = 5x - 2$	$(0, -2)$ is the coordinate of the y-intercept, so c (in the equation $y = mx + c$) will be -2
b) $y = 5x + 2$ has a gradient of 5 Gradient of perpendicular line is $-1 \div 5 = -\frac{1}{5}$	Lines which are perpendicular will have gradients with a product of -1. So you want $5 \times m = -1$
Equation is $y = -\frac{1}{5}x + 7$	$(0, 7)$ is the coordinate of the y-intercept, so c will be 7

Example 2

Find the equation of the line perpendicular to $y + 4x = 10$ that passes through the point $(8, -2)$

$y + 4x = 10$ $y = 10 - 4x$ $y = -4x + 10$	First rearrange to get the equation in the form $y = mx + c$
Gradient of perpendicular line is $-1 \div -4 = \frac{1}{4}$ $y = \frac{1}{4}x + c$	This line has a gradient of -4, so the perpendicular line will have a gradient of $\frac{1}{4}$ So you know it will be of the form $y = \frac{1}{4}x + c$
$-2 = \frac{1}{4} \times 8 + c$ $-2 = 2 + c$ $-4 = c$	You know that the perpendicular line passes through the point $(8, -2)$ so substitute these values into the equation to find the value of c.
Equation is $y = \frac{1}{4}x - 4$	

Fluency

1. Write down the equation of a line parallel to $y = 3x + 2$

2. Write down the equation of a line parallel to $y = 6x + 5$ that passes through the point $(0, 4)$

3. Find the equation of a line parallel to $2y + 3x = 5$ that passes through the point $(0, -1)$

4. Write down the gradient of a line perpendicular to:

    a) $y = 2x + 6$ b) $y = -5x + 4$ c) $y + 3x = 10$ d) $8y - x + 2 = 0$

5. Work out the equation of the line perpendicular to $y + 3x = 8$ that passes through the point $(0, -5)$

6. Find the equation of the line perpendicular to $y = -2x + 3$ that passes through the point $(-5, 10)$

7. Find the equation of the line perpendicular to $10y = 4x - 5$ that passes through the point $(4, 5)$

Further

1. Here are the equations of four straight lines:

    A $\boxed{y = 3x + 2}$ B $\boxed{y - 3x = 8}$ C $\boxed{y = -\frac{1}{3}x + 8}$ D $\boxed{y = 8x - 3}$

    a) Which line goes through the point $(3, 21)$?   (1 mark)

    b) Which lines have the same y-intercept?   (1 mark)

    c) Which lines are parallel?   (2 marks)

    d) Which lines are perpendicular?   (2 marks)

2. Two lines have the equations $3y = x + 12$ and $5y + 2x = 20$

    Determine if the lines are perpendicular.   (3 marks)

3. A straight line, l, passes through $A(4, 3)$ and $B(-2, 9)$

    a) Work out the equation of line l in the form $y = mx + c$ (2 marks)

    b) Work out the equation of a line perpendicular to l that goes through the midpoint of AB.   (3 marks)

4. Line p passes through $(-5, 0)$ and $(1, -3)$

    Line q passes through $(2, 7)$ and $(1, 1)$

    Are lines p and q perpendicular? Justify your answer.   (3 marks)

5. P, Q and R have coordinates $(5, 10)$, $(12, -4)$ and $(9, a)$ respectively. PQ is perpendicular to PR.

    Work out the value of a.   (4 marks)

Foundations

Solve: a) $x^2 + 5x + 6 = 0$ b) $x^2 - 7x + 12 = 0$ c) $x^2 + 3x - 10 = 0$

Facts

Quadratic graphs have equations of the form $y = ax^2 + bx + c$. The shape of a quadratic graph is called a **parabola**, a symmetrical U-shaped graph. The line of symmetry of the graph will have an equation of the form $x = p$ for some constant p.

If $a > 0$, the parabola will look like this:

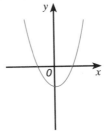

If $a < 0$, the parabola will look like this:

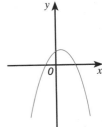

You can find the **y-intercept** of a quadratic graph by putting $x = 0$ into the equation.

You can find the **roots** of a quadratic graph by solving the equation $y = 0$. This will tell you the points where the curve crosses the x-axis.

The **turning point**, or **vertex** of the curve, is the minimum or maximum point of the parabola. You can find this coordinate by completing the square (see unit 2.13) and using your knowledge of transforming graphs (see unit 2.9).

Focus

Example

Sketch the graph of $y = x^2 - 6x - 7$, showing:

a) the coordinates of the y-intercept

b) where the graph crosses the x-axis

c) the coordinates of the turning point

d) the line of symmetry of the curve

a) When $x = 0$, $y = 0 - 0 - 7$ So y-intercept is $(0, -7)$	Set $x = 0$ to find the coordinates of the y-intercept.
b) When $y = 0$, $x^2 - 6x - 7 = 0$ $(x - 7)(x + 1) = 0$ $x = 7$, $x = -1$ The graph crosses the x-axis at $(7, 0)$ and $(-1, 0)$	Solve by factorising to find the roots. Some graphs just touch the x-axis once, e.g. $y = x^2 - 6x + 9$ touches the x-axis at $(3, 0)$
c) $y = x^2 - 6x - 7$ $y = (x - 3)^2 - 9 - 7$ $y = (x - 3)^2 - 16$ Turning point is at $(3, -16)$	Completing the square tells you the graph is a translation of $y = x^2$ by 3 units to the right and 16 units down. This also tells you that the line of symmetry has equation $x = 3$

d)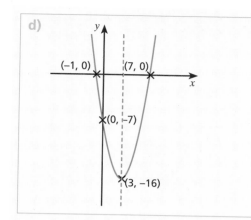

You can use the points you have worked out to sketch the curve.

The line of symmetry of the curve is shown by the vertical dashed line.

Fluency

1 Given $y = x^2 + 6x + 8$

a) Find the coordinates of the y-intercept.

b) Solve $x^2 + 6x + 8 = 0$ to find where the graph crosses the x-axis.

c) Complete the square to find the coordinates of the turning point of the graph of $y = x^2 + 6x + 8$

d) State the equation of the line of symmetry of the graph.

e) Sketch the graph, labelling all the key features.

2 Use the same steps as in question 1 to sketch the graphs of:

a) $y = x^2 + 2x - 15$ b) $y = x^2 - 49$

3 Given $y = -x^2 - 3x + 4$

a) Find the coordinates of the y-intercept.

b) Solve $-x^2 - 3x + 4 = 0$ to find where the graph crosses the x-axis.

c) By rewriting the equation as $y = -1(x^2 + 3x - 4)$, complete the square to find the coordinates of the turning point of the graph of $y = -x^2 - 3x + 4$

d) Sketch the graph, labelling all the key features.

Further

1 Given $y = x^2 + 16x + 64$

a) Work out the coordinates of the y-intercept. (1 mark)

b) Solve $x^2 + 16x + 64 = 0$

What does this tell you about the graph? (1 mark)

c) Sketch the graph, labelling all key features. (2 marks)

2 Sketch the graph of $y = 2x^2 + 11x + 12$, labelling all key features. (4 marks)

3 Given $y = x^2 + 4x + 10$

a) Try to solve the equation $x^2 + 4x + 10 = 0$ using the quadratic formula or by completing the square. What happens? (1 mark)

b) What does this tell you about the graph? (1 mark)

c) Complete the square to find the coordinates of the turning point. (2 marks)

d) Sketch the graph of $y = x^2 + 4x + 10$ (2 marks)

2.8 Other functions

Foundations

Work out: a) 3^2 b) 3^{-2} c) 2^{-3}

Facts

Exponential graphs have equations of the form $y = k^x$

For example, $y = 2^x$ represents exponential growth, whilst $y = 3^{-x}$ represents decay.

The graphs get closer and closer to the x-axis but do not touch it.

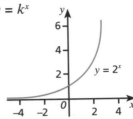
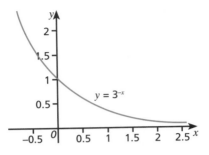

You need to recognise the shape and know the key features of the three **trigonometric graphs**.

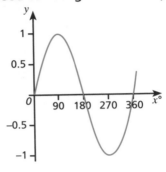
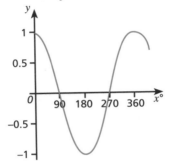
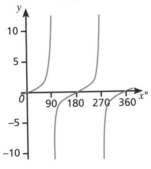

$y = \sin x$

Has period 360°
Maximum value = 1, Minimum value = –1
Crosses the x-axis at 0°, 180°, 360°, etc.

$y = \cos x$

Has period 360°
Maximum value = 1, Minimum value = –1
Crosses x-axis at 90°, 270°, etc.

$y = \tan x$

Has period 180°
Has no minimum or maximum value
Crosses the x-axis at 0°, 180°, 360°, etc.

Focus

Example 1

a) Complete the table of values for $y = 2^x$

x	–1	0	1	2	3
y					

b) Draw the graph of $y = 2^x$

c) Use your graph to estimate the value of x when y = 3

a)

x	–1	0	1	2	3
y	0.5	1	2	4	8

To find y, substitute the x values into the equation $y = 2^x$

$2^{-1} = 0.5$, $2^0 = 1$, $2^1 = 2$, $2^2 = 4$, $2^3 = 8$

b)

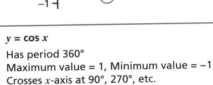

Plot the coordinates from the table and join with a smooth curve. Remember that the graph doesn't touch the x-axis.

c) From the graph, x = 1.6

Draw a horizontal line through y = 3 so that it touches the curve. Then use the graph to read the corresponding x value, as shown by the black dashed lines on the graph in part b).

Example 2
a) Use a graph to work out the value of sin 30°
b) Which other angles between 0° and 360° have the same sine as 30°?
c) Use a graph to estimate the solutions to sin x = −0.4

a) 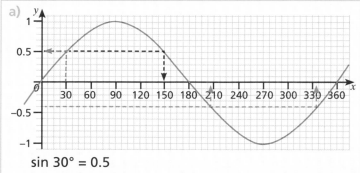 sin 30° = 0.5	Find 30 on the *x*-axis. Draw a line up to the curve and read off the corresponding *y* value.
b) sin 150° is also equal to 0.5	Start from 0.5 on the *y*-axis and draw a horizontal line to meet the curve. The first time it meets is at 30°. The second time is the other solution, as shown by the black dashed lines in the graph in part a). You could also work this out using the symmetry of the curve.
c) Solutions are *x* ≈ 205° and *x* ≈ 335°	Find −0.4 on the *y*-axis. Draw a horizontal line until it touches the curve. Find all solutions between 0° and 360°, as shown by the green dashed lines in the graph in part a).

Fluency

1 a) Complete the table of values for $y = 3^x$

x	−1	0	1	2	3
y					

   b) Draw the graph of $y = 3^x$

   c) Use your graph to estimate a solution to the equation $3^x = 16$

2 For this question, you will need a copy of the graph of $y = \cos x$

   Use the graph to find estimates of the solutions to these equations, in the interval 0° < *x* < 360°

   a) cos *x* = 0.6   b) 2cos *x* = −0.8

3 For this question, you will need a copy of the graph of $y = \tan x$

   Use the graph to find estimates of the solutions to these equations, in the interval 0° < *x* < 360°

   a) tan *x* = 1.4   b) tan *x* = −0.5

4 Which of these values cannot be the sine of an angle?   0   −0.9   1.2 $-\frac{2}{3}$ 5

Further

1 Here is part of the graph with equation $y = ab^x$

   The points with coordinates (0, 6), (1, 24) and (2, *c*) lie on the graph.

   Work out the values of *a*, *b* and *c*.   (3 marks)

2 a) Sketch the graph of $y = \sin x$ for 0° < *x* < 720°   (2 marks)

   b) Use your graph to estimate all the solutions to the equation sin *x* = 0.3 in the range 0° < *x* < 720°   (2 marks)

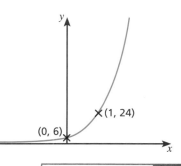

Other functions   39

2.9 Transformations of graphs

Foundations

Sketch the graphs of: **a)** $y = x^2$ **b)** $y = \cos x$ **c)** $y = \dfrac{1}{x}$

Facts

For a graph $y = f(x)$, $y = f(x) + a$ represents a **translation** by the vector $\begin{pmatrix} 0 \\ a \end{pmatrix}$

$y = f(x + a)$ represents a **translation** by the vector $\begin{pmatrix} -a \\ 0 \end{pmatrix}$

For a graph $y = f(x)$, $y = -f(x)$ represents a **reflection in the x-axis** and $y = f(-x)$ represents a **reflection in the y-axis**.

Focus

Example 1

The graph of $y = f(x)$ is shown.

Sketch the graphs of:

a) $y = f(x - 2)$

b) $y = -f(x)$

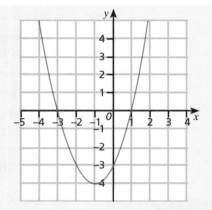

a) 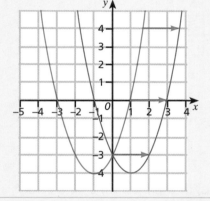	$f(x - 2)$ is a translation, two units to the right. So each point on the graph moves two units horizontally to the right.
b) 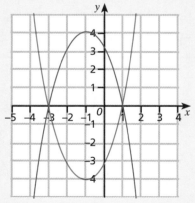	$-f(x)$ is a reflection in the x-axis. The parts that were above the x-axis will now be below, and the parts that were below the x-axis will now be above.

Example 2

Here is the graph of $y = f(x)$

The point A(3, 5) is on the graph.

What are the coordinates of the new position of A when the graph is transformed as follows?

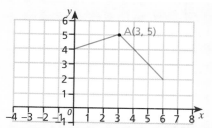

a) $y = -f(x)$ b) $y = f(x) - 2$ c) $y = f(x + 8)$

a)	(3, −5)	−f(x) is a reflection in the x-axis, so the x value will remain the same whilst the y value will be the negative of its current value.
b)	(3, 3)	f(x) − 2 is a translation down by two units, so all the points on the graph move down two units. This means the x value stays the same, but the y value is reduced by 2
c)	(−5, 5)	f(x + 8) is a translation of eight units to the left. The y value doesn't change but the x value is reduced by 8

Fluency

1 Match each equation to the correct transformation.

a) $y = f(x + 2)$ b) $y = f(x) + 2$ c) $y = f(x − 2)$ d) $y = f(x) − 2$

A Translation 2 units up   **B** Translation 2 units down   **C** Translation 2 units to the left   **D** Translation 2 units to the right

2 The diagram shows the graph $y = f(x)$

The point A(3, 1) lies on the graph $y = f(x)$

Sketch the graphs with the given equations, each time showing the coordinates of the point corresponding to A.

a) $y = f(-x)$ b) $y = f(x + 1)$

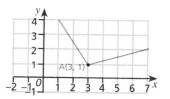

3 Below is the graph of $y = f(x)$

The coordinates of the minimum point on the curve are (−1, −6)

Write down the coordinates of the minimum point on the curve with the equation:

a) $y = f(x) − 4$
b) $y = f(x + 3)$
c) $y = f(-x)$

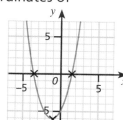

4 The graph $y = f(x)$ is shown on the grid. The graph labelled A is a translation of $y = f(x)$

Write down the equation of A.

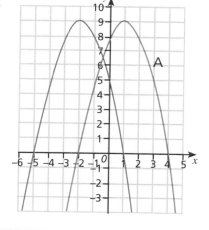

Further

1 The graph of $y = f(x)$ intercepts the x-axis at (−3, 0), (1, 0) and (4, 0). Write down the coordinates of the points where these graphs intercept the x-axis.

a) $y = f(-x)$ (2 marks)   b) $y = f(x − 1)$ (2 marks)

2 On the same axes, sketch the graphs of $y = \sin x$ and $y = \sin x + 2$ for $0° < x < 360°$ (3 marks)

3 On the same axes, sketch the graphs of $y = \cos x$ and $y = \cos (x + 90)$ for $0° < x < 360°$ (3 marks)

4 A graph $y = f(x)$ has a turning point at (2, 1)

Work out the coordinates of the turning point of the graph $y = f(x + 2) − 3$ (2 marks)

Foundations

Find the area of a trapezium with height 8 cm and parallel sides 10 cm and 12 cm.

Facts

The **gradient** of a straight line, given by $\frac{\text{change in } y}{\text{change in } x}$, represents a **rate of change**. For example, on a **speed–time graph**, the gradient is the rate of change of speed with respect to time, which is **acceleration**.

If you want to estimate the gradient at a point on a **curve**, you can draw a **tangent** to the curve (a straight line that just touches a curve at a given point) and calculate the gradient of the tangent.

> Gradient is covered in detail in unit 3.3

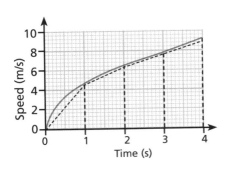

The area under a speed–time graph is the **distance** travelled. When the graph is a curve, you can estimate the area by splitting it into triangles, rectangles and trapezia. You can then work out the area of each part separately and add them together.

Focus

Example

Here is a velocity–time graph for a toy aeroplane.

a) Work out an estimate for the distance travelled by the plane in 4 seconds using four strips of equal width.

b) Is your answer to part a) an overestimate or an underestimate of the actual distance travelled? Justify your answer.

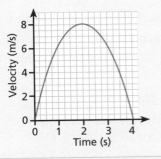

a) 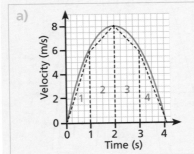	First split the area into strips to make triangles and trapezia. Label each part and then work out the areas.
Section 1: area = $\frac{1}{2} \times 1 \times 6 = 3$ Section 4: area = 3	Sections 1 and 4 have the same area. They are both triangles with base 1 and height 6 units.
Section 2: area = $\frac{1}{2}(6 + 8) \times 1 = 7$ Section 3: area = 7	Sections 2 and 3 are both trapezia with parallel sides of length 6 and 8 and a height of 1 unit.
Distance travelled = 3 + 3 + 7 + 7 = 20 m	Now add the areas together to get your estimate.
b) Underestimate as the areas of the four sections are all below the curve, so the actual area is greater.	Make sure you justify your answer.

Fluency

1. Here is a speed–time graph for a funfair ride.

   a) Work out the acceleration during each section.

   b) Work out the total distance travelled.

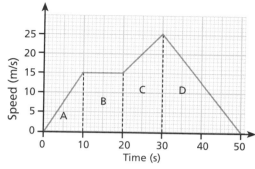

2. The speed–time graph shows the journey of a bike.

   a) Work out an estimate for the distance the bike travelled in the first 6 seconds using three strips of equal width.

   b) Is your answer to part a) an underestimate or an overestimate? You must justify your answer.

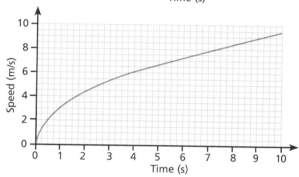

3. Here is a velocity–time graph for a remote-control helicopter.

   a) After how many seconds was the acceleration equal to 0?

   b) Work out the distance travelled during the first 3 seconds.

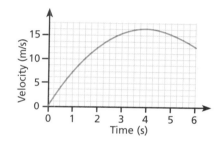

Further

1. The diagram shows the graph of $y = 16 - x^2$

   a) Work out an estimate of the area between the curve and the x-axis between $x = 0$ and $x = 3$, using three strips of equal width.   (3 marks)

   b) How could you improve your estimate in part a)?   (1 mark)

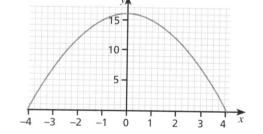

2. The diagram shows the graph of $y = x^3 + 2x^2 + 1$

   a) Estimate the gradient of the curve at the point where $x = 0.5$ (2 marks)

   b) Estimate the area under the curve between $x = -1$ and $x = 0$ (2 marks)

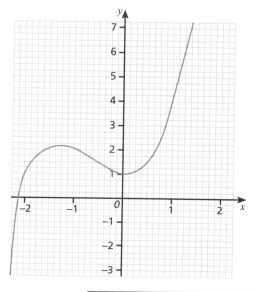

2.11 Equations of circles

Foundations

1. Find the gradient of the line segment joining the points (4, −2) and (2, 8)
2. Find the gradient of the line perpendicular to $y = \frac{1}{4}x - 1$

Facts

The **equation of a circle** with centre at (0, 0) and radius r is given by $x^2 + y^2 = r^2$

You know from circle theorems that the radius is always perpendicular to a tangent to the circle at a given point. This helps you to work out the equation of a tangent to a circle.

See units 4.3 and 4.4 for circle theorems.

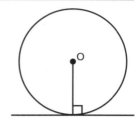

Focus

Example 1
The equation of a circle is $x^2 + y^2 = 16$

a) State the coordinates of the centre of the circle.
b) Work out the length of the radius of the circle.
c) Does the point (3, 4) lie on the circle? Show your working.

a) Centre is at (0, 0)	Remember that $x^2 + y^2 = r^2$ is the equation of a circle centred at the origin.
b) $r^2 = 16$, so $r = 4$	Here, $r^2 = 16$, so you can use this to find the radius.
c) $x^2 + y^2 = 3^2 + 4^2 = 9 + 16 = 25$ $25 \neq 16$ so the point doesn't lie on the circle	To check if the point is on the circle, you need to substitute $x = 3$ and $y = 4$ into the equation.

Example 2
Work out the equation of the tangent to the circle $x^2 + y^2 = 25$ at the point (3, 4)

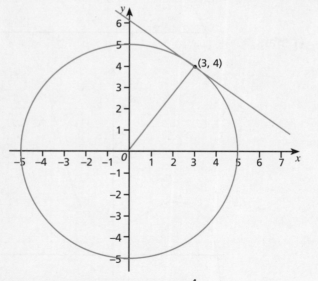

The gradient of the radius is $\frac{4}{3}$

The gradient of the tangent will be $-\frac{3}{4}$

To find the equation of a straight line, you first need the gradient.

To find this, first find the gradient of the radius from the centre to (3, 4)

The tangent will be perpendicular to the radius so its gradient is the negative reciprocal of $\frac{4}{3}$ (see unit 2.6).

$y = -\frac{3}{4}x + c$	Now you know the gradient, you know the general form of the equation.
$4 = -\frac{3}{4} \times 3 + c$ $4 = -\frac{9}{4} + c$ $\frac{25}{4} = c$	You can substitute in $x = 3$ and $y = 4$ to find the value of c.
So the equation is $y = -\frac{3}{4}x + \frac{25}{4}$	This equation could be written as $4y = -3x + 25$

Fluency

1. A circle has equation $x^2 + y^2 = 36$
   a) Find the length of the radius of the circle.
   b) Does the point (4, 2) lie on the circle? Show your working.
   c) The point P with coordinates (4, y) lies on the circle. Find two possible values of y.

2. A circle has centre (0, 0) and radius 5
   a) Write down the equation of the circle.
   b) Does the point (4, −3) lie on the circle? Show your working.

3. Write down the equation of the circle shown.

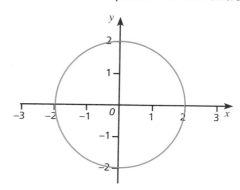

4. Sketch the circle $x^2 + y^2 = 49$, labelling all the axes intercepts.

5. The point (0, −8) lies on a circle with centre (0, 0). Find the equation of the circle.

Further

1. AB is the diameter of a circle where A = (4, 3) and B = (−4, −3)
   a) Work out the centre of the circle.   (2 marks)
   b) Work out the equation of the circle.   (2 marks)

2. A circle is centred on the origin. The point (5, −12) lies on the circle.
   Work out the equation of the circle.   (3 marks)

3. A circle has equation $x^2 + y^2 = 20$
   a) Work out the length of the radius of the circle, giving your answer in surd form.   (1 mark)
   b) Work out the equation of the tangent to the circle at the point (2, 4)   (3 marks)

4. A circle has equation $x^2 + y^2 = 13$
   a) Work out the equation of the tangent to the circle at the point (−2, 3)   (3 marks)
   b) Work out the coordinates of the point where the tangent crosses the x-axis.   (1 mark)

2.12 Quadratic equations

Foundations

Solve: **a)** $x^2 - 7x + 10 = 0$ **b)** $x^2 - 3x - 18 = 0$ **c)** $x^2 + 12x + 32 = 0$

Facts

Factorising is one method of solving quadratic equations. However, if the quadratic expression does not factorise, you can use the **quadratic formula** instead.

For a general quadratic equation of the form $ax^2 + bx + c = 0$, the solutions can be found using the formula

$$x = \frac{-b \pm \sqrt{b^2 - 4ac}}{2a}$$

| Note that you use the formula twice (once with the + and once with the –) in order to get both solutions. |

You may need to rearrange an equation into the form $ax^2 + bx + c = 0$ before using the formula.

Focus

Example 1

Solve the equation $2x^2 + 5x - 4 = 0$ using the quadratic formula. Give your answer correct to 2 decimal places.

$2x^2 + 5x - 4 = 0$ $a = 2$, $b = 5$ and $c = -4$	First identify a, b and c from your equation, paying attention to the signs.
$x = \dfrac{-b \pm \sqrt{b^2 - 4ac}}{2a}$	Next write out the quadratic formula.
$x = \dfrac{-5 \pm \sqrt{5^2 - 4 \times 2 \times -4}}{2 \times 2}$	Substitute the values of a, b and c.
$x = \dfrac{-5 + \sqrt{5^2 - 4 \times 2 \times -4}}{2 \times 2} = 0.64$	Then carefully input the first calculation with + into your calculator ($-5 + \sqrt{\ldots}$ on the numerator).
$x = \dfrac{-5 - \sqrt{5^2 - 4 \times 2 \times -4}}{2 \times 2} = -3.14$	Repeat with the second calculation ($-5 - \sqrt{\ldots}$ on the numerator).
The solutions are $x = 0.64$ and $x = -3.14$	In surd form, the answers would be $x = \dfrac{-5 + \sqrt{57}}{4}$ and $\dfrac{-5 - \sqrt{57}}{4}$

Example 2

A rectangle has width x cm and length $x + 6$ cm.

The area of the rectangle is 65 cm²

a) Show that $x^2 + 6x - 65 = 0$

b) Work out the value of x.

x cm

$x + 6$ cm

a)	Area $= x \times (x + 6)$	The area of a rectangle is length × width.
	$x(x + 6) = 65$	Here, you know the area is 65, so you can form an equation.
	$x^2 + 6x = 65$	Now expand, simplify and rearrange to get into the form $ax^2 + bx + c = 0$
	$x^2 + 6x - 65 = 0$	

b) $a = 1, b = 6, c = -65$	You can use the quadratic formula to solve this equation. Identify the values of a, b and c.
$x = \dfrac{-6 \pm \sqrt{6^2 - 4 \times 1 \times -65}}{2 \times 1}$	Use the formula.
$x = 5.6$ or $x = -11.6$	Remember to apply it twice.
$x = 5.6$ (to 1 d.p.)	In the context of this question, x represents a length and so cannot be negative. This means that you can discount the negative solution.

Fluency

1 Solve the equations. Give your answers to 2 decimal places.

a) $2x^2 + 6x - 1 = 0$

b) $4x^2 + x - 7 = 0$

c) $x^2 - 2x - 10 = 0$

2 Solve the equations. Give your answers in surd form.

a) $x^2 + 2x - 7 = 0$

b) $x^2 + 6x - 11 = 0$

c) $x^2 - 4x - 1 = 0$

3 Solve $5x^2 - 3 = 6x$, giving your answer to 3 significant figures.

4 Solve $11x = -x^2 + 3x + 3$, giving your answer correct to 1 decimal place.

5 A rectangle is 12 cm longer than it is wide.

The area of the rectangle is 48 cm²

a) Show that $x^2 + 12x - 48 = 0$

b) Work out the dimensions of the rectangle.

Further

1 The diagram shows a hexagon made from two rectangles.

The area of the hexagon is 33 cm²

a) Show that $2x^2 + 10x - 15 = 0$ (2 marks)

b) Work out the value of x correct to 2 decimal places. (2 marks)

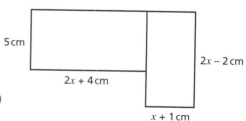

2 Here is a right-angled triangle.

a) Use Pythagoras' theorem to show that $x^2 - 14x - 6 = 0$ (2 marks)

b) Work out the value of x. (2 marks)

c) Work out the perimeter of the triangle. (1 mark)

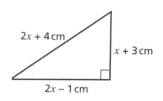

3 The diagram shows a trapezium.

The trapezium has area 75 cm²

Work out the value of x. (4 marks)

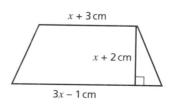

2.13 Completing the square

Foundations

1 Expand the brackets.

   a) $(x + 4)(x + 4)$ **b)** $(x + 12)^2$ **c)** $(x - 5)^2$

2 Solve the equations.

   a) $(x + 3)(x - 2) = 0$ **b)** $(x - 5)(x - 5) = 0$ **c)** $x^2 - 10x + 24 = 0$

Facts

Some quadratic expressions can be written as perfect squares of binomials.

$x^2 + 6x + 9 \equiv (x + 3)^2$ ⟵

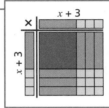

You can see this using algebra tiles.

One x^2 tile, 6 x tiles and 9 ones tiles can be arranged to form a square.

Other quadratic expressions are not perfect squares, but can be compared to the closest perfect square expression.

This process is called 'completing the square'.

$x^2 + 6x + 11 \equiv (x + 3)^2 + 2$ ⟵

$x^2 + 6x + 5 \equiv (x + 3)^2 - 4$ ⟵

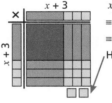

$x^2 + 6x + 11$
$\equiv x^2 + 6x + 9 + 2$
$\equiv (x + 3)^2 + 2$

Here are the two 'extra' tiles.

$x^2 + 6x + 5$
$\equiv x^2 + 6x + 9 - 4$
$\equiv (x + 3)^2 - 4$

You would need four more tiles to 'complete the square'.

When you rewrite a quadratic expression like $x^2 + 6x + 5$ as $(x + 3)^2 - 4$, you are writing it in the form $(x + a)^2 + b$. In this case $a = 3$ and $b = -4$

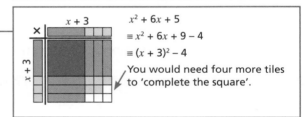

Focus

Example 1

Write $x^2 + 8x + 10$ in the form $(x + a)^2 + b$

$x^2 + 8x + 10 \equiv (x + 4)^2 + b$	Start by working out a. You know $a = 4$ as when you expand the brackets of $(x + 4)^2$ you will get two terms of $+4x$, which total to $8x$.
$x^2 + 8x + 10 \equiv x^2 + 8x + 16 + b$	Expand $(x + 4)^2$ to give $x^2 + 8x + 16$
$10 = 16 + b$	You know $10 = 16 + b$ by comparing the constant terms in the identity.
$b = -6$	Solve the equation to work out b.
$x^2 + 8x + 10 \equiv (x + 4)^2 - 6$	You can now write the expression in the required form.

When you write an expression $x^2 + px + q$ in the form $(x + a)^2 + b$, you need to halve the coefficient of the x term to find a, i.e. $a = \frac{p}{2}$

Example 2

Write $x^2 - 6x - 5$ in the form $(x + a)^2 + b$

$x^2 - 6x - 5 \equiv (x - 3)^2 + b$	Start by working out a. $a = -6 \div 2 = -3$
$x^2 - 6x - 5 \equiv x^2 - 6x + 9 + b$	Expand $(x - 3)^2$ to give $x^2 - 6x + 9$
$-5 = 9 + b$	Compare the constants.
$b = -14$	Solve the equation to work out b.
$x^2 - 6x - 5 \equiv (x - 3)^2 - 14$	Write the expression in the required form.

Example 3

Solve the equation $x^2 - 4x - 8 = 0$, giving your answers in the form $p + q\sqrt{r}$

$x^2 - 4x - 8 \equiv (x - 2)^2 + b$ $x^2 - 4x - 8 \equiv x^2 - 4x + 4 + b$ $-8 = 4 + b$ $b = -12$	Start by writing $x^2 - 4x - 8$ in completed square form as in Examples 1 and 2.
$(x - 2)^2 - 12 = 0$	Rewrite the equation in completed square form.
$(x - 2)^2 = 12$	Rearrange to (expression)^2 = number
$x - 2 = \pm\sqrt{12}$	Square root both sides. You need to include $\pm\sqrt{12}$ so you get both solutions to the quadratic equation.
$x = 2 \pm\sqrt{12}$	Rearrange to find x.
$x = 2 \pm 2\sqrt{3}$	Write the expression in the required form.

You could also solve this question using the quadratic formula. See unit 2.12

For more about surds, see unit 1.4

Fluency

1. Are these expressions perfect squares? If so, write in the form $(x + a)^2$

   a) $x^2 + 8x - 16$ b) $x^2 - 8x - 16$ c) $x^2 + 8x + 16$ d) $x^2 - 8x + 16$

2. Write these expressions in the form $(x + a)^2$, where a is an integer.

   a) $x^2 + 12x + 36$ b) $x^2 - 10x + 25$ c) $x^2 - 4x + 4$

3. Write these expressions in the form $(x + a)^2 + b$, where a and b are integers.

   a) $x^2 + 8x + 10$ b) $x^2 + 8x + 20$ c) $x^2 + 8x - 10$

   d) $x^2 + 4x + 7$ e) $x^2 - 4x + 20$ f) $x^2 - 6x - 2$

4. a) Find the values of p and q such that $x^2 + 10x + 6 \equiv (x + p)^2 + q$

   b) Hence or otherwise, solve the equation $x^2 + 10x + 6 = 0$

5. Solve the equation $x^2 - 6x + 1 = 0$, giving your answers in simplified surd form.

Further

1. Write $2x^2 + 16x + 5$ in the form $a(x + p)^2 + q$ (3 marks)

   Start by writing the expression as $2(x^2 + 8x) + 5$ and then write $x^2 + 8x$ in completed square form.

2. The expression $x^2 + 14x + 30$ has a minimum value.

   Complete the statements.   (3 marks)

   Start by writing the expression in completed square form.

   The minimum value of $x^2 + 14x + 30$ occurs when $x = $ ....

   The minimum value of $x^2 + 14x + 30$ is ....

3. Work out the coordinates of the turning point of the curve with equation $y = x^2 + 2x + 5$ (3 marks)

   See unit 2.7 for more information about turning points.

2.14 Simultaneous equations with a quadratic

Foundations

1. Solve the simultaneous equations: $5x + 6y = 34$, $y = x + 2$
2. Solve: a) $x^2 - 9x + 20 = 0$ b) $x^2 - 2x - 8 = 0$

Facts

When you solve a pair of linear simultaneous equations, you get one solution consisting of an x and a y value. This represents the point of intersection of the straight lines given by the equations.

For example, solving $3x + 2y = 17$ and $4x - y = 30$ gives $x = 7$ and $y = -2$

The lines meet at the point $(7, -2)$ where $x = 7$ and $y = -2$

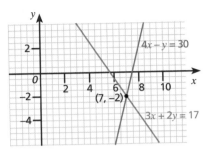

When you solve a pair of simultaneous equations where one of them is quadratic, you often get two solutions. This is because a straight line can cross a curve in two places.

For example, solving $y = x + 3$ and $y = x^2 + 3x$ gives two sets of solutions, $x = -3$, $y = 0$ and $x = 1$, $y = 4$

You can see that the graphs intersect at the points $(-3, 0)$ and $(1, 4)$

You usually solve simultaneous equations like these by substituting the linear equation into the quadratic equation. You may have to rearrange it first.

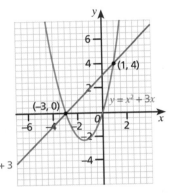

Focus

Example 1
Solve the simultaneous equations.

$$y = x^2 + 2$$
$$y + 3x = 0$$

$y = x^2 + 2$ (1) $y + 3x = 0$ (2)	Label the equations to help make your solution clear. Notice equation (1) is quadratic and equation (2) is linear.
$y + 3x = 0$ $y = -3x$	To substitute, you need to make either x or y the subject of the linear equation.
Put this in equation (1)	Then substitute this expression for y into the non-linear equation.
$-3x = x^2 + 2$	
$0 = x^2 + 3x + 2$	Rearrange to get a quadratic in a form you can solve.
$0 = (x + 2)(x + 1)$	Solve this quadratic to get two x values.
So $x = -2$, $x = -1$	
$y = -3x$ When $x = -2$, $y = -3 \times -2 = 6$ When $x = -1$, $y = -3 \times -1 = 3$	Now use the linear equation to find the corresponding y value for each x value.
So the solutions are $x = -2$, $y = 6$ and $x = -1$, $y = 3$	

Example 2

Solve the simultaneous equations: $x^2 + y^2 = 20$

$x + y = 6$

$x^2 + y^2 = 20$ (1) $x + y = 6$ (2)	First label the equations.
$x + y = 6$ $x = 6 - y$ (3)	To substitute, you need to make either x or y the subject of the linear equation.
Put this in equation (1) $(6 - y)^2 + y^2 = 20$	Then substitute this expression for x into the non-linear equation.
$36 - 6y - 6y + y^2 + y^2 = 20$ $36 - 12y + 2y^2 = 20$ $2y^2 - 12y + 16 = 0$ $y^2 - 6y + 8 = 0$	Expand, simplify and rearrange to get a quadratic in a form you can solve.
$(y - 4)(y - 2) = 0$ $y = 4, y = 2$	Solve this quadratic to get two y values.
Put these in equation (3) When $y = 4$, $x = 6 - 4 = 2$ When $y = 2$, $x = 6 - 2 = 4$	Now use the linear equation to find the corresponding x value for each y value.
So the solutions are $x = 2, y = 4$ and $x = 4, y = 2$	

Fluency

Solve each pair of simultaneous equations.

a) $x^2 + y^2 = 20$ and $x = 2y$

b) $y - x - 1 = 0$ and $y = x^2 + x$

c) $xy = 24$ and $x + 2 = y$

d) $y = x + 2$ and $y - 3x^2 = 0$

e) $x^2 + y^2 = 45$ and $5x - 21 = 3y$

Further

1 Solve each pair of simultaneous equations.

   a) $4y + x = 3$ and $x + \frac{2}{y} = 1$ (4 marks)

   b) $y = \frac{4}{x}$ and $y + x = 5$ (4 marks)

   c) $5x^2 - xy = 6$ and $y - 3 = 2x$ (4 marks)

2 The graphs of $x^2 + y^2 = 25$ and $y = 7 - x$ intersect at the points A and B.

   a) Work out the coordinates of A and B. (3 marks)

   b) Work out the exact length of the chord AB. (2 marks)

Foundations

Work out $\sqrt[3]{12 - 5x}$ when: **a)** $x = 1$ **b)** $x = -2$ **c)** $x = 2.8$

Give your answers to 2 decimal places.

Facts

You don't have a method or formula for solving an equation like $x^3 - 7x - 12 = 0$

You can confirm the location of a solution by looking for a **change of sign**.

If you substitute $x = 3$ into $x^3 - 7x - 12$, you get $27 - 21 - 12 = -6$

If you substitute $x = 4$ into $x^3 - 7x - 12$, you get $64 - 28 - 12 = 24$

The value of the expression has changed from negative to positive (this is the change of sign). The value you want, 0, is in between -6 and 24. This means the x value you need is between 3 and 4

You then need to rearrange the equation to form an **iterative formula** (this is usually given in the exam question).

Here is one way of rearranging the formula above:

$$x^3 - 7x - 12 = 0$$
$$x^3 = 7x + 12$$
$$x = \sqrt[3]{7x + 12}$$

The formula is then written using subscript notation $x_{n+1} = \sqrt[3]{7x_n + 12}$

You then choose a sensible starting value (somewhere between 3 and 4 in this case) as x_1, your starting value.

You then work out x_2 using the formula and then repeat the process, using x_2 as x_n to get x_3, and so on. This is shown in Example 1 below. If you have chosen a good starting value, the successive values of x_n get closer and closer together and **converge** to the root you are looking for.

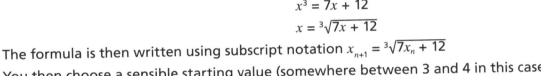

Focus

Example 1

Using $x_{n+1} = \sqrt[3]{7x_n + 12}$ and $x_1 = 3.5$, work out the values of x_2, x_3 and x_4 each to 5 decimal places.

$x_{n+1} = \sqrt[3]{7x_n + 12}$ $x_2 = \sqrt[3]{7x_1 + 12}$ $x_2 = \sqrt[3]{7 \times 3.5 + 12} = 3.31714$	Replacing n with 1 gives the formula you need to start with. Use $x_1 = 3.5$ to find x_2
$x_3 = \sqrt[3]{7x_2 + 12}$ $= 3.27791$	Now repeat the process, using x_2 to find x_3
$x_4 = \sqrt[3]{7x_3 + 12}$ $= 3.26936$	Then use x_3 to find x_4 The easiest way to do this is by using a key like "ANS" on your calculator. You can then enter 3.5 as your first answer, press = and then enter $\sqrt[3]{7 \text{ ANS} + 12}$ Next press = to get x_2, then press = to get x_3, and so on. If you keep pressing =, with this example you see the answers get closer and closer together.

Example 2

a) Show that $x_{n+1} = \sqrt{5x_n - 3}$ can be used to solve the equation $x^2 - 5x + 3 = 0$

b) Using $x_1 = 4$, find a solution to the equation correct to 2 decimal places.

a) $x^2 - 5x + 3 = 0$	You need to rearrange to make x the subject. Since the iterative
$x^2 = 5x - 3$	formula given has a square root in it, this suggests making the first
$x = \sqrt{5x - 3}$	x the subject.
$x_{n+1} = \sqrt{5x_n - 3}$	Then write this using the correct notation.
	You can still do the second part of the question even if you are not sure how to do the first part.
b) $x_2 = \sqrt{5x_1 - 3}$	Replacing n with 1 gives the formula you need to start with.
$x_2 = \sqrt{5 \times 4 - 3} = 4.12...$	Use $x_1 = 4$ to find x_2
$x_3 = \sqrt{5x_2 - 3} = 4.19...$	Now repeat the process, using x_2 to find x_3
$x_4 = 4.240...$	Keep repeating the process until two solutions in a row give the
$x_5 = 4.266...$	same answer to 2 decimal places.
$x_6 = 4.281...$	
$x_7 = 4.290...$	
$x_8 = 4.295...$	You don't have to do as many iterations as this in an exam. This
$x_9 = 4.298...$	example is just to give you practice with the process.
$x = 4.30$ to 2 decimal places	

You could also use the quadratic formula to find the solutions to this equation.

Fluency

1. Show that $x^3 - 5x - 4 = 0$ has a solution between $x = 2$ and $x = 3$

2. Given the iterative formula $x_{n+1} = 6 - \dfrac{4}{x_n}$, with $x_1 = 1.5$, find the values of x_2, x_3 and x_4

3. a) Show that the equation $6x^2 - 7x - 2 = 0$ can be rearranged to give the iterative formula $x_{n+1} = \sqrt{\dfrac{7x_n + 2}{6}}$

   b) Use the formula together with $x_1 = 1$ to find a solution to the equation correct to 2 decimal places.

4. a) Show that the equation $x^3 + 2x - 1 = 0$ has a solution between $x = 0$ and $x = 1$

   b) Show that $x^3 + 2x - 1 = 0$ can be rearranged to give $x = \frac{1}{2}(1 - x^3)$

   c) Starting with $x_1 = 0.5$, use the iterative formula $x_{n+1} = \frac{1}{2}(1 - x_n^3)$ three times to estimate a solution to $x^3 + 2x - 1 = 0$

Further

1. Which of the following formulae cannot be found by rearranging the equation $x^3 + 6x - 4 = 0$?

   A $\quad x = \dfrac{4 - x^3}{6}$ B $\quad x = 4 + 6x^3$ C $\quad x = \sqrt[3]{4 - 6x}$ D $\quad \dfrac{x^3}{6} + 4 = x$

2. a) Show that $x^3 + 7x - 5 = 0$ can be rearranged to give $x = \dfrac{5}{(x^2 + 7)}$ (2 marks)

   b) Use the iterative formula $x_{n+1} = \dfrac{5}{x_n^2 + 7}$ together with $x_1 = 1$, to find x_2, x_3 and x_4 (2 marks)

   c) Substitute your answer for x_4 into $x^3 + 7x - 5 = 0$ and comment on the accuracy of x_4 as an estimate of the root of the equation.   (1 mark)

3. Explain why using $x_1 = 1$ as the first value is not suitable with the iterative formula $x_{n+1} = \sqrt{10 - 7x_n}$ (2 marks)

2.16 Two or more inequalities

Foundations

On a set of axes, sketch the graphs: **a)** $x = 3$ **b)** $y = -2$ **c)** $y = x$ **d)** $y = 2x - 1$

Facts

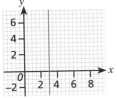

An inequality can be represented as a region on a pair of axes.

Here is the line with equation $x = 3$

On the line, all the points have an x-coordinate of 3

To the left of the line, all points have an x-coordinate less than 3, so you can describe that region as $x < 3$

To the right of the line, all points have an x-coordinate greater than 3, so you can describe that region as $x > 3$

When using number lines, you use empty or filled circles to distinguish between inequalities involving $<$, $>$ or $\leqslant$, $\geqslant$

When working with regions, you can use solid or dashed lines to distinguish the two cases. Use a dashed line for $<$ or $>$ (the line is not included in the region) and use a solid line for $\leqslant$ or $\geqslant$ (the line is included in the region).

Focus

Example 1

Show the region defined by the inequalities $x > -1$ and $y \leqslant 2$

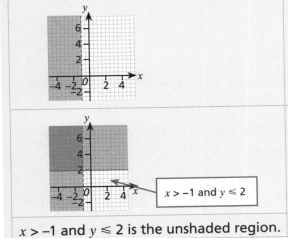

	To start with, sketch your axes.
	Then draw the line $x = -1$ (dashed as it is not included)
	It can be easier to shade the unwanted region. Since you want $x > -1$, you want the region to the right of the line, so you can shade the left-hand side.
	Next draw the line $y = 2$ (solid)
	Since you want the region where $y \leqslant 2$, you want the part below the line. Therefore, shade the region above.
$x > -1$ and $y \leqslant 2$	The region you want is left unshaded.
$x > -1$ and $y \leqslant 2$ is the unshaded region.	Identify your choice of region clearly.

Example 2

Show the region where $3x + 4y > 12$

$3x + 4y = 12$ When $x = 0$, $y = 3$ When $y = 0$, $x = 4$	First draw the line $3x + 4y = 12$ using a dashed line. Setting x and y equal to zero gives you two key points through which to draw the line, or you could use a table of values.
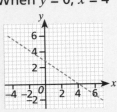	

Choosing (2, 4), which is above the line, as a test point gives $3x + 4y = 3 \times 2 + 4 \times 4 > 12$ and this is in the region.	To determine which side to shade in, choose a test point on one side of the line. (2, 4) is an easy point to work with here.
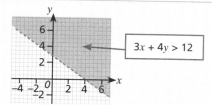	Since (2, 4) satisfies the inequality, you can shade above the line to show the region where $3x + 4y > 12$ This question asks you to 'Show the region' rather than the unwanted region. Always make it clear what your shading means.

Fluency

1 For parts a)–e) shade the **unwanted** regions and leave the described region clear.

a) $x > 2$ and $y \geqslant 1$

b) $x < 5$, $x \geqslant -2$ and $y \leqslant 4$

c) $x \leqslant 1.5$, $y > -2$ and $y \leqslant 2.5$

d) $y < 2x$

e) $x + 2y \geqslant 6$

2 Draw graphs to show the following. Label with the letter R the region which satisfies the given set of inequalities.

a) $2x + 5y \leqslant 10$, $x \geqslant 0$, $y \geqslant -4$

b) $2x + 3y \leqslant 6$, $1 < x < 3$

Further

1 For each given graph, state the inequality which satisfies the unshaded region.

a)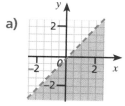

(1 mark)

b)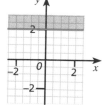

(1 mark)

c)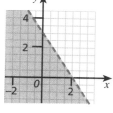

(1 mark)

d)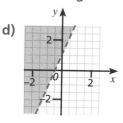

(1 mark)

2 A point P has integer coordinates and lies in the region given by:

$y < 3$, $1 < x < 5$ and $2y \geqslant x$

a) Draw a diagram to show the region in which P lies.   (3 marks)

b) Write down all the possible coordinates of the point P.   (1 mark)

3 Write down the three inequalities that define the unshaded region.   (3 marks)

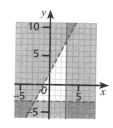

2.17 Quadratic inequalities

Foundations

Solve the equations:
   a) $x^2 + 3x + 2 = 0$
   b) $x^2 + 3x - 10 = 0$
   c) $x^2 - 8x + 15 = 0$

Facts

Linear inequalities have one solution set. For example, $2x + 1 > 9$ is true when $x > 4$

Quadratic inequalities may have one or two solution sets. For example, $x^2 \leqslant 9$ is true for all values of x between 3 and −3 inclusive. However, $x^2 > 9$ is true both when $x > 3$ (for example, $5^2 = 25$, which is greater than 9) and when $x < -3$ (for example, $(-4)^2 = 16$, which is greater than 9).

The solution sets can also be written using **set notation**.

For $x^2 \leqslant 9$ this would be $\{x: -3 \leqslant x \leqslant 3\}$. This is read as 'The values of x such that x is between −3 and 3'.

For $x^2 > 9$ this would be $\{x: x < -3\} \cup \{x: x > 3\}$, using $\cup$ to represent the **union** of the two sets that tell you where the inequality is true.

To decide which values are in the solution set(s) of a quadratic inequality, you should always sketch a graph to help. The end point(s) of the set(s) are known as the **critical values** and can be found by factorisation, as shown in the examples below.

Focus

Example 1
Solve the inequality $x^2 - 9x + 14 \geqslant 0$, giving your answer in set notation.

When $x^2 - 9x + 14 = 0$ $(x - 7)(x - 2) = 0$ Critical values are $x = 7$ and $x = 2$	First set the quadratic equal to zero and solve the equation to find the critical values.
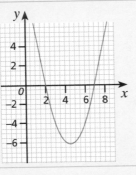	Next sketch the graph of $y = x^2 - 9x + 14$
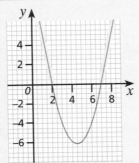	You want the areas where the y values are greater than or equal to zero. Identify this on the graph.
The solution set is $x \leqslant 2$, $x \geqslant 7$	Write the solutions using inequality notation.
In set notation $\{x: x \leqslant 2\} \cup \{x: x \geqslant 7\}$	Write the solutions using set notation.

Example 2

Find the set of values of x for which $x^2 - 5x > 24$ and $2x + 10 < 28$

$x^2 - 5x > 24$ $x^2 - 5x - 24 > 0$ When $x^2 - 5x - 24 = 0$ $(x - 8)(x + 3) = 0$ $x = 8$, $x = -3$	You need so solve both the given inequalities. Start by rearranging the quadratic to a solvable form. Find the critical values.
	Sketch the graph and identify the required section – the parts where the y values are greater than 0
$x < -3$, $x > 8$	Give your answers using inequalities.
$2x + 10 < 28$ $2x < 18$ $x < 9$	Now solve the linear inequality.
	Drawing a number line can help you to see which values of x satisfy both inequalities.
Final answer: $x < -3$, $8 < x < 9$	The parts that satisfy both inequalities are where $x < -3$ and where $8 < x < 9$

Fluency

1 Solve each inequality below, giving your answers in set notation.

   a) $x^2 - x - 30 > 0$

   b) $x^2 - 2x - 35 \leqslant 0$

   c) $x^2 \geqslant 100$

   d) $x^2 < x + 20$

   e) $2x^2 + 7x + 5 > 0$

2 $x > 3 \cup x < -4$ is the solution to which inequality?

   $x^2 - x - 12 > 0$ $x^2 - x - 12 < 0$ $x^2 + x - 12 < 0$ $x^2 + x - 12 > 0$

Further

1 Solve the inequality $x^2 - 4x + 1 > 0$, giving your answer in surd form. (3 marks)

2 Work out the set of values of x to satisfy both $x^2 > 100$ and $x^2 + 8x - 48 \leqslant 0$ (4 marks)

3 Work out the integer values of x which satisfy $x^2 - 7x - 11 < 0$ (4 marks)

2.18 Geometric sequences

Foundations

Find the next term in each sequence.

a) 3, 7, 11, 15, … b) 3, 6, 12, 24, … c) 14, 7, 3.5, 1.75, …

Facts

A **geometric sequence** is one in which each term is found by multiplying the previous term by the same number. This **constant multiplier** is also called the **common ratio**. The common ratio can be an integer, a fraction or even a surd.

For example, in the sequence 4, 12, 36, 108, … each term is three times the size of the previous term, so this is a geometric sequence with common ratio 3

The nth term of a geometric sequence with first term a and common ratio r is ar^{n-1}

Focus

Example 1
Work out the next two terms of each sequence.

a) 2, 8, 32, 128, …

b) 12, 3, $\frac{3}{4}$, $\frac{3}{16}$, …

c) 2, $2\sqrt{2}$, 4, $4\sqrt{2}$, …

a) 2, 8, 32, 128 $\times 4$ $\times 4$ $\times 4$ The common ratio is 4	First you need to find the common ratio. You can do this by dividing any successive pair of terms. $2 \times r = 8$ so $r = 8 \div 2 = 4$ $8 \times r = 32$ so $r = 32 \div 8 = 4$
$128 \times 4 = 512$ $512 \times 4 = 2048$	So you can get the next two terms by multiplying by 4
b) 12, 3, $\frac{3}{4}$, $\frac{3}{16}$ $\times \frac{1}{4}$ $\times \frac{1}{4}$ $\times \frac{1}{4}$ The common ratio is $\frac{1}{4}$	Find the common ratio by dividing: $12 \times r = 3$ so $r = 3 \div 12 = \frac{1}{4}$ It is easier to work with fractions than decimals.
$\frac{3}{16} \times \frac{1}{4} = \frac{3}{64}$ $\frac{3}{64} \times \frac{1}{4} = \frac{3}{256}$	So you can get the next two terms by multiplying by $\frac{1}{4}$
c) 2, $2\sqrt{2}$, 4, $4\sqrt{2}$ $\times \sqrt{2}$ $\times \sqrt{2}$ $\times \sqrt{2}$ The common ratio is $\sqrt{2}$	Find the common ratio by dividing: $2 \times r = 2\sqrt{2}$ so $r = 2\sqrt{2} \div 2 = \sqrt{2}$
$4\sqrt{2} \times \sqrt{2} = 8$ $8 \times \sqrt{2} = 8\sqrt{2}$	So you can get the next two terms by multiplying by $\sqrt{2}$

Example 2

The second term of a geometric sequence is 10 and the fifth term is 1250

Work out the first term of the sequence.

2nd 3rd 4th 5th 10 ? ? 1250 × r × r × r	To get from the second term to the fifth term, you need to multiply by the common ratio three times.
$10 \times r \times r \times r = 1250$ $10r^3 = 1250$ $r^3 = 125$ $r = 5$ First term = $10 \div 5 = 2$	

Fluency

1 Which of these sequences are geometric?

A | 3 | 6 | 9 | 12 | 15 |

B | 2 | 6 | 12 | 36 | 108 |

C | 8 | 4 | 2 | 1 | 0.5 |

D | 10 | 20 | 30 | 40 | 50 |

2 Find the next two terms of each geometric sequence.

a) 5, 15, 45, 135, … b) 4, −8, 16, −32, … c) 6, 2, $\frac{2}{3}$, $\frac{2}{9}$, …

d) 9, −3, 1, −$\frac{1}{3}$, … e) 4, $4\sqrt{3}$, 12, $12\sqrt{3}$, …

3 The nth term of a geometric sequence is $3 \times 4^{n-1}$

Work out the first four terms of the sequence.

4 The nth term of a geometric sequence is $2 \times \left(\frac{1}{2}\right)^{n-1}$

Work out the first four terms of the sequence.

Further

1 Here is a geometric sequence: 3, 12, 48, 192, ….

a) Write down the common ratio. (1 mark)

b) Write down the next two terms. (1 mark)

c) Work out a rule for the nth term of the sequence. (2 marks)

d) Work out the value of the 12th term divided by the 8th term. (1 mark)

2 Work out the next two terms in this sequence. 3, $6\sqrt{2}$, 24, $48\sqrt{2}$, … (2 marks)

3 Work out a rule for the nth term of each sequence.

a) 6, −12, 24, −48, … (2 marks)

b) 3, $3\sqrt{7}$, 21, $21\sqrt{7}$, … (2 marks)

4 A ball is dropped from 10 m. Each time it bounces to 80% of its previous height.

a) Work out the height of the ball after the first four bounces. (2 marks)

b) Explain why this forms a geometric sequence. (1 mark)

c) Work out the height of the ball after the sixth bounce. (2 marks)

d) Do you think this is a reasonable model? (1 mark)

2.19 Quadratic sequences

Foundations

1 Find the first four terms of each sequence.

   a) $5 - 6n$ **b)** $n^2 + 2$

2 Find the rule for the nth term of the sequences that start:

   a) 3, 7, 11, 15, 19, ...   **b)** 8, 6, 4, 2, 0, ...

Facts

In a **linear sequence**, the difference between each pair of successive terms is the same.

In a **quadratic sequence**, the **second differences** are equal.

9   13   19   27   ...

+ 4   + 6   + 8 ← These are the first differences.

+ 2   + 2 ← Second differences are equal.

The rule for the nth term of a quadratic sequence will always contain a term in n^2. The coefficient of n^2 will be half of the second difference.

Focus

Example 1

Write down the next two terms in the sequence that starts 4, 15, 32, 55, 84, ...

4 15 32 55 84 + 11 + 17 + 23 + 29 + 6 + 6 + 6	First you need to work out the differences between the terms. Then work out the second differences to help.
6th term: 84 + 35 = 119	The next difference in the sequence will be 29 + 6 = 35
7th term: 119 + 41 = 160	The following difference will be 35 + 6 = 41

Example 2

A quadratic sequence has nth term $n^2 + 3n - 1$

Work out the first four terms in the sequence.

$n^2 + 3n - 1$ $1^2 + 3(1) - 1 = 3$ $2^2 + 3(2) - 1 = 9$ $3^2 + 3(3) - 1 = 17$ $4^2 + 3(4) - 1 = 27$ So the sequence starts 3, 9, 17, 27	To find the first four terms, you need to substitute $n = 1, 2, 3$ and 4 into the nth term rule.

Example 3

Find, in terms of n, a rule for the nth term of the sequence that starts 2, 10, 24, 44, …

2   10   24   44
  + 8   + 14   + 20
    + 6   + 6
	First work out the first differences and the second differences.
	
	Half of 6 is 3. This tells you that the nth term rule includes $3n^2$

Sequence: 2 10 24 44 $3n^2$: 3 12 27 48 −1 −2 −3 −4	Write out the sequence for $3n^2$ and subtract each term from your sequence to see what's left. This gives a linear sequence.
Difference is −1 nth term is −1n	Find the nth term rule for the linear sequence.
nth term is $3n^2 - n$	The given sequence is the sum of the quadratic part and the linear part.

Fluency

① Write down the next two terms in each quadratic sequence.

   a) 2, 9, 18, 29, 42, …

   b) 0, 1, 6, 15, 28, …

② Find the first four terms in the sequences given by the rules:

   a) $n^2 + 2n$

   b) $2n^2 - 3$

   c) $(n - 1)^2$

③ The nth term of the sequence 1, 4, 9, 16, … is given by n^2

   Use this to work out the rule for the nth term of these sequences.

   a) 2, 8, 18, 32

   b) 2, 5, 10, 17

   c) −2, 1, 6, 13

④ The nth term of the quadratic sequence that starts 3, 9, 17, 27, … is given by which expression?

   $n^2 - 3n + 1$ $n^2 - 3n - 1$ $n^2 + 3n - 1$ $n^2 + 3n + 1$

Further

① The nth term of a sequence is $2n^2 + 3n - 4$

   Work out the difference between the third and fifth terms.   (2 marks)

② Work out, in terms of n, a rule for the nth term of each sequence.

   a) 5, 11, 19, 29, … (3 marks)

   b) 3, 11, 23, 39, … (3 marks)

   c) 15, 19, 25, 33, … (3 marks)

③ A quadratic sequence starts 5, 9, 15, 23, …

   a) Work out the nth term for the sequence.   (3 marks)

   b) Which term in the sequence has the value 59?   (2 marks)

Facts

Two quantities are in **direct proportion** when as one increases or decreases, the other increases or decreases at the same rate. The **ratio** between the two quantities is constant.

For example, if the cost of one packet of stickers is £1.20, you can represent the relationship between the number of packets bought and the cost using a table.

Packets	0	1	2	3	4
Cost	0	£1.20	£2.40	£3.60	£4.80

You can also use a **double number line**:

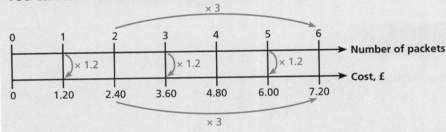

As the ratio is constant, you can use multiplication and division to find missing values.

For example, if 8 boxes contain 280 nails, 80 boxes will contain 280 × 10 = 2800 nails, as 80 = 8 × 10

Two boxes will contain 280 ÷ 4 = 70 nails, as 2 = 8 ÷ 4

The graph of a direct proportion relationship is a **straight line** that goes through the **origin**:

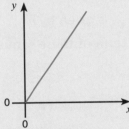

The equation of the line will be $y = kx$ for some constant k.

In an **inverse proportion** relationship, as one variable increases the other decreases by the same factor. For example, if 8 machines take 3 hours to produce 1000 items, then working at the same rate 4 machines would take 3 × 2 = 6 hours and 80 machines would take 3 ÷ 10 = 0.3 hours = 18 minutes

The graph of an inverse proportion relationship is a curve like this:

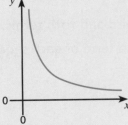

The equation of the line will be $y = \frac{k}{x}$ for some constant k.

Relationships involving **growth and decay** involve repeated use of the same ratio.

For example, if a population, P, increases by 12% a year, then after n years the population will be $P \times 1.12^n$

If the population decreases by 12% a year, then after n years the population will be $P \times 0.88^n$

Practice

1 Three cups of coffee cost £5.70

Complete the table to show the cost of buying different numbers of cups of coffee.

Number of cups	1	3	4	
Cost		£5.70		£20.90

2 At a petrol station, 6 litres of fuel cost £10

Calculate the cost of:

a) 54 litres   b) 15 litres   c) 100 litres

3 Tick the graphs that show a direct proportion relationship.

A 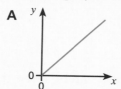   **B** 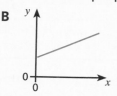   **C** 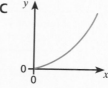   **D** 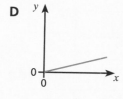   **E**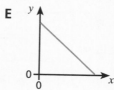

4 Which table, A or B, shows a direct proportion relationship?

A

x	5	10	15
y	8	12	16

B

x	5	10	15
y	16	32	48

5 p is directly proportional to q.

Complete the table.

p	3	5	10	40		
q		13			156	260

6 It takes 12 people 9 hours to build a wall.

How long would it take the following number of people to build the same size of wall?

a) 24 people   b) 4 people   c) 16 people

What assumption have you made?

7 x is inversely proportional to y.

Complete the row for xy. What do you notice?

x	1	4	10	24
y	40	10	4	1.$\dot{6}$
xy				

8 A photocopier makes 35 copies per minute.

a) How many copies can be made in one hour?

b) How long will it take the photocopier to make 7000 copies?

9 a is inversely proportional to b. When $a = 12$, $b = 9$

Find b when $a = 10$

10 There are 200 weeds in a garden.

How many weeds will there be in one week's time if:

a) the number of weeds increases by 5% a day?

b) the number of weeds decreases by 5% a day?

Foundations

1 You are given that $a : b = 2 : 5$ and $b : c = 3 : 2$

Find the ratio $a : b : c$ in its simplest form.

2 Ali, Tiff and Zach share some money in the ratio $5 : 4 : 3$

Zach receives £2.50 less than Ali. How much money did they share?

Facts

When working with **equivalent ratios**, if $a : b = c : d$ then $\frac{a}{b} = \frac{c}{d}$ and $\frac{a}{c} = \frac{b}{d}$

Bar models can help you to see relationships between parts more clearly and they are useful to represent problems. For example, if the ratio of red counters to yellow counters in a box is $4 : 3$, it can be modelled as:

Red

Yellow

> Your model may look slightly different to this. This is fine as long as it models the situation accurately.

If half of the red counters are removed and 10 more yellow counters are added, the model can be altered to:

Red

Yellow | 10

Focus

Example 1

Huda, Rob and Junaid share some money.

Rob receives $\frac{1}{10}$ of the money and Huda and Junaid share the rest in the ratio $2 : 3$

What percentage of the money does Huda receive?

Let the total amount of money shared be 100% $\frac{1}{10}$ of 100% = 10%	Rob receives 10% of the money.
90% of the money is shared between Huda and Junaid. 90% ÷ 5 = 18% 18% × 2 = 36%	Share 90% in the ratio 2 : 3, so five parts altogether.
Huda receives 36% of the money.	Huda receives two parts.

Example 2

A box contains only apples and oranges.

The ratio of apples to oranges in the box is $5 : 2$ and there are 30 apples in the box.

Some oranges are added to the box so the ratio of apples to oranges is now $10 : 9$

How many oranges were added to the box?

30 ÷ 5 = 6, so each part of the ratio represents six pieces of fruit. 6 × 2 = 12	The number of apples in the box is 30, so you can work out the number of pieces of fruit represented by each part of the ratio.
To begin with, there were 30 apples and 12 oranges.	Write down how many of each piece of fruit there were initially.
$30 : 12 + n = 10 : 9$	Let the number of oranges added be n.
$\dfrac{30}{12 + n} = \dfrac{10}{9}$	Write the ratio as an equation involving fractions.
$270 = 120 + 10n$ $150 = 10n$ $15 = n$ 15 oranges were added to the box.	Solve the equation.

Fluency

1 Kath and Rhys share some sweets. The ratio of the number of sweets that Kath has to the number of sweets that Rhys has is 4 : 3

Kath gives five sweets to Rhys. The ratio of Kath's sweets to Rhys's sweets is now 1 : 1

How many sweets did they share?

2 Some staff and students go on a school trip.

The ratio of students to adults is 12 : 1

The ratio of Year 10 students to Year 11 students is 4 : 5

What fraction of all the people on the trip are Year 11 students?

3 A factory makes boxes.

All of the boxes are either green or blue.

All of the boxes are either large or small.

The ratio of the number of green boxes to the number of blue boxes is 3 : 2

For the green boxes, the number of large boxes : the number of small boxes = 5 : 3

What percentage of the boxes made at the factory are green and small?

4 Ali and Bev share some sweets in the ratio 4 : 3

Ali receives a sweets and Bev receives b sweets.

Ed and Marta share three times as many sweets as Ali and Bev share.

They share their sweets in the ratio 3 : 2

Ed receives c sweets and Marta receives d sweets.

Work out $a : b : c : d$

5 The ratio of Bobbie's age to Lida's age is 5 : 3

Two years ago, the ratio of their ages was 7 : 4

How old is Lida?

Further

1 A bag contains only blue or red cubes. The probability of choosing a red cube is 0.8

Some blue cubes are added. The probability of choosing a red cube is now $\frac{5}{8}$

Work out the ratio of the number of cubes at the start to the number of cubes after the blue cubes are added. Give your answer in its simplest form.   (3 marks)

2 $(a - b) : (a + b) = k : 1$

Work out a formula for a in terms of b and k.   (3 marks)

3 Given that $x^2 : (3x - 4) = 2 : 1$, work out the possible values for x.   (3 marks)

4 Liquid A has a density of 3.5 g per cm³

The ratio of the density of liquid A to the density of liquid B is 5 : 8

The two liquids are mixed in the ratio 1 : 4

Work out the density of the mixture.   (3 marks)

3.2 Direct and inverse proportion equations

Foundations

Given that $y = 5x^2$, work out:

a) the value of y when $x = 20$

b) the value of x when $y = 20$

c) the value of x when $y = 40$, giving your answer in surd form

Facts

Two quantities are in direct proportion when, as one increases, the other increases at the same rate.

You write 'y is directly proportional to x' as $y \propto x$. This can also be written as $y = kx$, where k is called the **constant of proportionality**.

The graph of $y = kx$ is a straight line that passes through the origin.

Two quantities are in **inverse proportion** when, as one increases, the other decreases at the same rate.

This is written as $y \propto \frac{1}{x}$ or $y = \frac{k}{x}$. The graph of $y = \frac{k}{x}$ is a reciprocal curve.

One quantity can be directly proportional or inversely proportional to the square, cube, square root, etc. of another quantity. If you form an equation connecting the variables, it can be used to find unknown values.

Focus

Example 1

y is directly proportional to x. When $y = 144$, $x = 48$

a) Work out the value of y when $x = 35$

b) Work out the value of x when $y = 35$

a) $y \propto x$ $y = kx$ $144 = 48k$ $k = \frac{144}{48} = 3$	Form and solve an equation to find the constant of proportionality using the values given in the question.
$y = 3x$	Use your value of k to form an equation connecting y and x.
$y = 3 \times 35$ $y = 105$	Substitute in the value of x to find the value of y.
b) $y = 3x$ $35 = 3x$	Use the equation found in part a), this time substituting the given value of y.
$x = \frac{35}{3}$	Solve to find x. You can leave your answer as an exact fraction.

Example 2

r is inversely proportional to the square of t.
When $r = 150$, $t = 0.6$

Work out the value of t when $r = 6$ and $t \geqslant 0$

$r \propto \frac{1}{t^2}$ $r = \frac{k}{t^2}$	Form and solve an equation to find the constant of proportionality, writing 'the square of t' as t^2.
$150 = \frac{k}{0.6^2}$ $150 \times 0.6^2 = k$	Work out the value of k by substituting in the values of r and t.
$k = 54$ $r = \frac{54}{t^2}$	Rewrite the equation with the value of k you found.
$6 = \frac{54}{t^2}$	Substitute in $r = 6$
$t^2 = \frac{54}{6}$ $t^2 = 9$ $t = \sqrt{9}$ $t = 3$	Rearrange the equation to work out the value of t.

Fluency

1 g is directly proportional to h. When $g = 300$, $h = 75$

   a) Write an equation connecting g and h.

   b) Find the value of g when $h = 8$

   c) Find the value of h when $g = 6$

2 p is inversely proportional to s. When $p = 9$, $s = 4$

   a) Find the value of p when $s = 1.8$

   b) Find the value of s when $p = 30$

3 The graph shows how y varies with x.

   a) Work out the value of y when $x = 52$

   b) Work out the value of x when:

   i) $y = 100$

   ii) $y = 4$

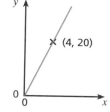

4 p varies directly with r. When $p = 14$, $r = 3$

   a) Write an equation connecting p and r.

   b) Work out the value of p when $r = 48$

   c) Work out the value of r when $p = 5$, giving your answer as a fraction.

> 'Varies directly with' is another way of saying 'is directly proportional to'.

5 t varies with s. When $t = 24$, $s = 64$

   Write t in terms of s if:

   a) t is directly proportional to the square root of s

   b) t is inversely proportional to the cube root of s

   c) t is directly proportional to the cube of s

6 y is inversely proportional to the square of x. When $y = 350$, $x = 0.4$

   Calculate the value of x when:

   a) $y = 14$

   b) $y = 8$, giving your answer in surd form

Further

1 x is directly proportional to the cube root of y.

   z is inversely proportional to the square of x.

   When $x = 5$, $y = 8$ and $z = 3$

   Work out the value of z when $y = 3.375$ (4 marks)

2 a) In a circle, explain why the area is directly proportional to the square of its radius, stating the constant of proportionality.   (1 mark)

   b) The volume of a sphere varies with the cube of its radius.

   If the volume of a sphere with radius 5 cm is 524 cm³, calculate the volume of a sphere with radius 11 cm.   (3 marks)

3 m is inversely proportional to the square root of p. When $m = 2$, $p = 48$

   a) Show that $m = \dfrac{8\sqrt{3p}}{p}$ (3 marks)

   b) Work out the value of p when $m = 8\sqrt{5}$ (2 marks)

Foundations

Find the gradient of the line segment joining the points (2, –3) and (6, 5)

Facts

To estimate the **gradient at a point** on a curve, you can draw a **tangent** to the curve at the point. A tangent is a straight line that touches a curve at the point with the same gradient. You can then draw a right-angled triangle onto the tangent to work out the gradient, using the formula gradient $= \dfrac{\text{change in } y}{\text{change in } x}$

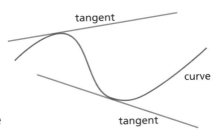

The gradient of a tangent can be interpreted as the instantaneous rate of change, so for a distance–time graph this would be the speed. For a speed–time graph, it would be the acceleration.

Focus

Example

The graph shows the speed of a car for the first 10 seconds of its journey.

a) Work out the average rate of change of speed between $t = 0\,$s and $t = 10\,$s

b) Interpret the average rate of change in the context of the question.

c) Estimate the rate of change at $t = 4\,$s

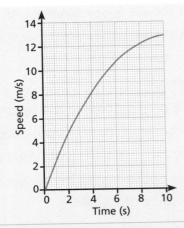

a) When $t = 0$, $s = 0$ and when $t = 10$, $s = 12.8$ $m = \dfrac{12.8 - 0}{10 - 0} = 1.28$	Use the graph to identify the speeds at $t = 0$ and $t = 10$ Substitute the coordinates into the gradient formula $m = \dfrac{y_2 - y_1}{x_2 - x_1}$
b) The average acceleration was 1.28 m/s²	The gradient of a speed–time graph represents acceleration.
c) 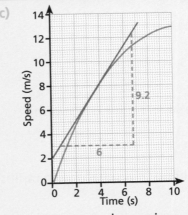	Draw a tangent at $t = 4$ Draw a right-angled triangle onto the tangent to work out the gradient.
Gradient $= \dfrac{\text{change in } y}{\text{change in } x} = \dfrac{9.2}{6}$ $= 1.5$ to 2 significant figures	The acceleration at $t = 4$ is approximately 1.5 m/s²

Fluency

1 The graph shows how the height of a ball fired vertically upwards changes over time.

a) i) Estimate the instantaneous rate of change at 4 seconds.

ii) Interpret the rate of change in the context of the question.

b) Work out the average rate of change between 1 and 3 seconds.

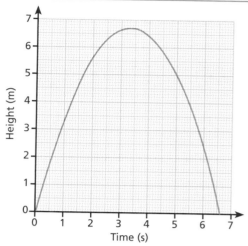

2 The distance–time graph below shows the journey of a cyclist over 5 minutes.

a) Work out the average speed of the cyclist during the first half of their journey.

b) i) Work out an estimate for the greatest speed reached by the cyclist on their journey in miles per hour.

> This will be the steepest part of the curve.

ii) Explain why your answer to part b) i) is an estimate.

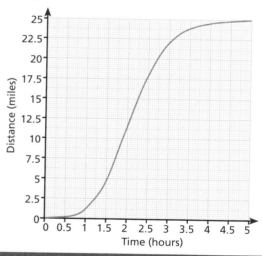

3 Seb throws a basketball. The graph below shows the height of the ball above the ground.

a) Estimate the speed of the ball at 1 second.

b) What can you say about the speed at 2.5 s?

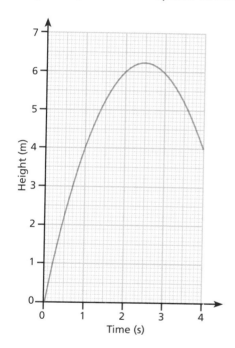

Further

The graph shows the temperature of a cup of tea as it cools in a room. The room is at a constant temperature.

a) Work out an estimate for the average rate at which the cup of tea cools between $t = 2$ and $t = 10$ (3 marks)

b) Work out an estimate for the instantaneous rate of change at 2 minutes. (3 marks)

c) Samira says, "The gradient of the curve will be negative for all values of time."

Do you agree with Samira? Explain your answer. (1 mark)

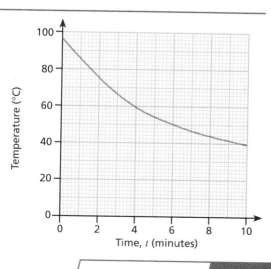

Facts

An **angle** is a measure of turn. Angles are measured in degrees (°), with 360° in a **full turn**.

As a straight line is half a turn, adjacent **angles on a straight line** add up to 180°

Here are some other key angles facts:

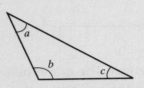

The angles in a triangle add up to 180°
$a + b + c = 180°$

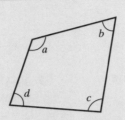

The angles in a quadrilateral add up to 360°
$a + b + c + d = 360°$

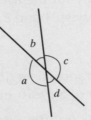

Vertically opposite angles are equal
$a = c$ and $b = d$

You also need to know these facts about angles formed when a **transversal line** cuts **parallel lines**:

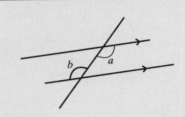

Alternate angles are equal
$a = b$

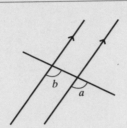

Corresponding angles are equal
$a = b$

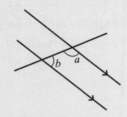

Co-interior angles add up to 180°
$a + b = 180°$

You should also know these key facts about angles in **polygons** (shapes with straight sides):

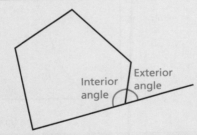

Interior angle • Exterior angle

- The exterior angles of a polygon always add up to 360°
- To find the sum of the interior angles of a polygon, you can split the shape into triangles from one vertex or use the formula:
  sum = $(n - 2) \times 180°$, where n is the number of sides of the polygon.
- The interior and exterior angles of a polygon lie on a straight line and so will always add up to 180°
- A polygon is **regular** if all its sides are equal in length and all its angles are equal in size.

Practice

1. Work out the sizes of the angles labelled with letters.

a)

b)

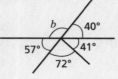

c)

147°
c

2 Work out the value of x in each of the diagrams.

a)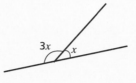

b)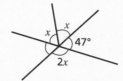

c)

3 Work out the size of the angle labelled with a letter in each diagram.

a)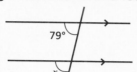

b)

c)

d)

4 Work out the values of v, w and x.
Give reasons for your answers.

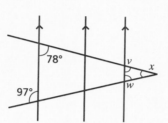

5 Are any of the pairs of line segments parallel?

a)

b)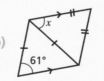

6 Calculate the value of x.

7 Work out the sizes of the angles marked with letters.

a)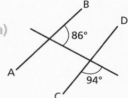

b)

8 A regular polygon has n sides. Work out the value of n if the size of each exterior angle is:

a) 30°   b) 15°   c) 22.5°

9 A regular polygon has n sides. Work out the value of n if the size of each interior angle is:

a) 108°   b) 144°   c) 162°

10 Work out the value of x in each diagram.

a)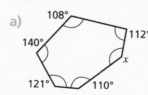

b)

c)

11 Work out the size of angle y.

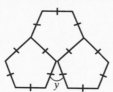

Facts

To describe the **transformation** of an **object** to an **image**, you need to state which transformation has occurred and the specific elements of that transformation.

To describe a **translation**, write the column vector $\binom{a}{b}$ to describe the horizontal ($\leftrightarrow$) and vertical ($\updownarrow$) movement of the shape. Remember, $\binom{2}{3}$ means 2 units right and 3 units up. $\binom{-2}{-3}$ means 2 units left and 3 units down.

For example:

A to B: Translation by the vector $\binom{0}{2}$

A to C: Translation by the vector $\binom{-3}{3}$

A to D: Translation by the vector $\binom{1}{-3}$

A to E: Translation by the vector $\binom{-2}{-1}$

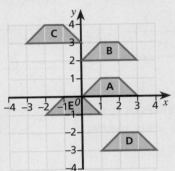

To describe a **reflection**, you need to state the equation of the line the shape has been reflected in.

A to B: Reflection in the line $x = 0$ (or the y-axis)

A to C: Reflection in the line $y = -1$

A to D: Reflection in the line $y = x$

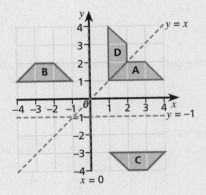

To describe a **rotation**, give the amount (in degrees) and direction of the turn, and the **centre of rotation**. You can use tracing paper to help you to perform or describe a rotation.

A to B: Rotation, 90° clockwise about (0, 0)

A to C: Rotation, 180°, centre (0, 1)

The direction is not needed for a turn of 180°

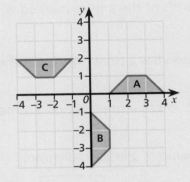

To describe an **enlargement**, you need to state the **centre** and the **scale factor** of enlargement.

A to B: Enlargement, scale factor 2, centre (2, 3)

A to C: Enlargement, scale factor $\frac{1}{3}$, centre (0, 3)

If you draw rays connecting at least two corresponding vertices on the object and the image, where they meet is the centre of enlargement.

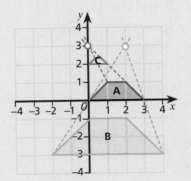

Practice

1 Describe the single transformation that maps:

  a) shape A to shape B

  b) shape A to shape C

  c) shape D to shape A

  d) shape C to shape E

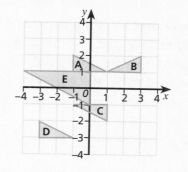

2 Describe the single transformation that maps:

  a) shape A to shape B

  b) shape A to shape C

  c) shape E to shape A

  d) shape B to shape F

  e) shape E to shape D

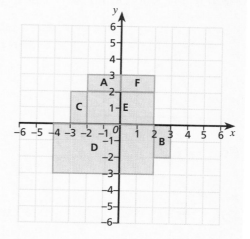

3 Faith is asked to describe fully the single transformation that maps shape P onto shape Q.

She says, "Reflect shape P in the line $y = 3$ and then reflect this shape in the line $x = 3.5$ to get shape Q."

Explain Faith's mistake and give the correct answer.

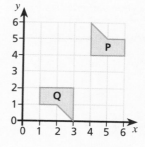

4 a) Describe fully the translation that maps square A to square B.

  b) Describe fully the reflection that maps square A to square B.

  c) Describe fully a rotation that maps square A to square B such that the centre of rotation is not the origin.

  d) Which of the transformations above is also a transformation that maps B to A?

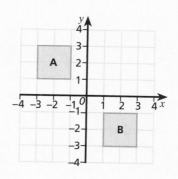

Facts

Trigonometry is the study of angles and side lengths in triangles. In right-angled triangles, it is helpful to label the sides of the triangles as the **hypotenuse** (opposite the right angle), **opposite** (opposite the angle you are working with) and **adjacent** (touching the angle you are working with), as shown.

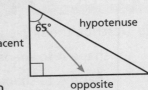

Trigonometry uses the **ratios** between the side lengths in right-angled triangles for different sizes of angles. These are:

$$\sin \theta = \frac{\text{opposite}}{\text{hypotenuse}} \qquad \cos \theta = \frac{\text{adjacent}}{\text{hypotenuse}} \qquad \tan \theta = \frac{\text{opposite}}{\text{adjacent}}$$

Sin, cos and tan are abbreviations of the words sine, cosine and tangent.

Here is how you would work out an unknown side, AB:

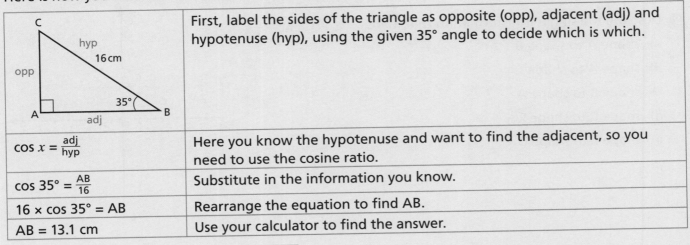

	First, label the sides of the triangle as opposite (opp), adjacent (adj) and hypotenuse (hyp), using the given 35° angle to decide which is which.
$\cos x = \frac{\text{adj}}{\text{hyp}}$	Here you know the hypotenuse and want to find the adjacent, so you need to use the cosine ratio.
$\cos 35° = \frac{AB}{16}$	Substitute in the information you know.
$16 \times \cos 35° = AB$	Rearrange the equation to find AB.
$AB = 13.1$ cm	Use your calculator to find the answer.

> Make sure your calculator is set up to work in degrees.

Here is how you would work out an unknown angle:

	First, label the triangle using the missing angle x to determine the labels.
$\tan x = \frac{\text{opp}}{\text{adj}}$	Use the labelling to decide which ratio you need to use. Here you know the opposite and adjacent, so you need to use the tangent ratio. Write down the ratio.
$\tan x = \frac{14}{22}$	Substitute in the information you know.
$x = \tan^{-1}\left(\frac{14}{22}\right)$ $x = 32.5°$	If you know a ratio, you use the inverse function on your calculator to find the angle. Here, the inverse of tangent is denoted as $\tan^{-1}$

You should know the exact values of the **trigonometric ratios** shown in the table.

> $\frac{1}{\sqrt{3}}$ can also be written as $\frac{\sqrt{3}}{3}$

	0°	30°	45°	60°	90°
sin	0	$\frac{1}{2}$	$\frac{\sqrt{2}}{2}$	$\frac{\sqrt{3}}{2}$	1
cos	1	$\frac{\sqrt{3}}{2}$	$\frac{\sqrt{2}}{2}$	$\frac{1}{2}$	0
tan	0	$\frac{1}{\sqrt{3}}$	1	$\sqrt{3}$	Undefined

When solving problems in right-angled triangles, you may also need to use Pythagoras' theorem, $a^2 + b^2 = c^2$, where a and b are the shorter sides and c is the hypotenuse.

Practice

1 Solve: a) $5x = 82.36$ b) $5 = \dfrac{82.36}{x}$ c) $5 = \dfrac{x}{82.36}$

2 Work out the lengths of the sides labelled with letters.

a)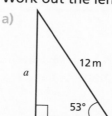

b)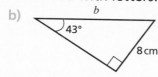

c)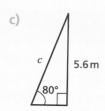

d)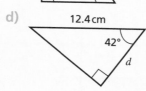

e)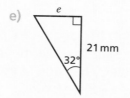

f)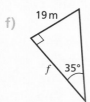

3 Work out the sizes of the angles labelled θ.

a)

b)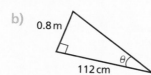

c)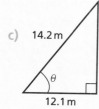

d)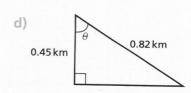

e)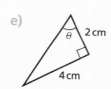

f)

4 Work out the value of p in these triangles.

a)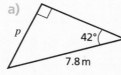
b)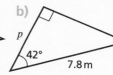
c)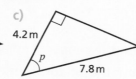
d)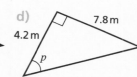
e)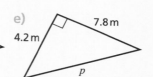

5 Work out the value of x in each of the diagrams.   a) 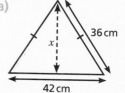   b)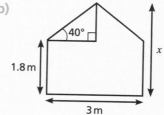

6 Calculate the length of BD.

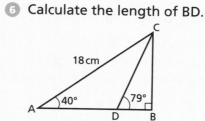

7 Without using a calculator, work out the exact values of x and y.   a) 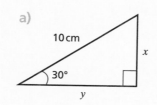   b)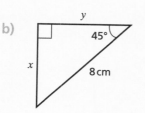

Foundations

A square has side length 6 cm. Find the new side length when the square is enlarged by:

a) scale factor 3

b) scale factor $\frac{1}{4}$

Facts

Enlarging an **object** with a **negative scale factor** inverts the shape about the centre of enlargement whilst resizing according to the numerical part of the scale factor. Object refers to the shape before a transformation and **image** refers to the shape after the transformation.

The example shows triangle ABC enlarged by scale factor –2 about the origin, O.

Drawing rays from each vertex of the triangle through the origin can help to identify the corresponding vertices of the image. The rays meet at the **centre of enlargement**. The image, triangle A'B'C', has side lengths twice as long as those of ABC. The distance from the centre of enlargement to a vertex on the image is twice the distance from the centre to the corresponding vertex on the object.

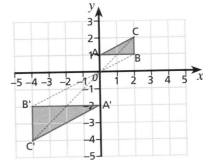

Focus

Example 1

Enlarge rectangle PQRS by scale factor –3, centre (–2, –1) and label the vertices of the image P', Q', R' and S'.

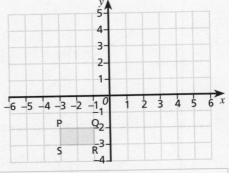

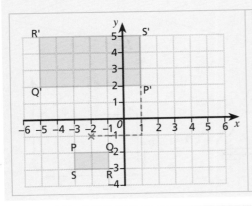

First plot the centre of enlargement (–2, –1) on the grid.

Work out the vector from the centre of enlargement to each vertex. In this example, the vector from the centre of enlargement to P is $\binom{-1}{-1}$. You need to enlarge the shape by –3, so multiply the vector by –3: $\binom{-1}{-1} \times -3 = \binom{3}{3}$

Use the vector $\binom{3}{3}$ from the centre of enlargement to find the position of vertex P'. Repeat this for each of the other vertices in order to enlarge the shape, ensuring each vertex is correctly labelled.

Example 2

Describe fully the single transformation that maps triangle JKL to triangle J'K'L'.

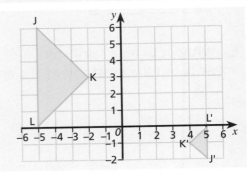

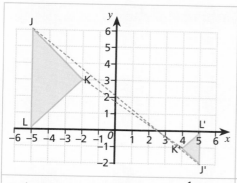

Since the size and orientation of J'K'L' is different to that of JKL, the transformation must be an enlargement with a negative scale factor.

Comparing corresponding side lengths JL = 6 and J'L' = 2 shows that the scale factor of enlargement must be $-\frac{1}{3}$

Draw rays between corresponding vertices to identify the centre of enlargement: (2.5, 0)

Enlargement, scale factor $-\frac{1}{3}$, centre (2.5, 0)	Describe the transformation fully – type, scale factor and centre of enlargement.

Fluency

1 Enlarge shape A by scale factor −2, centre 0.

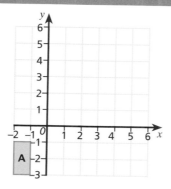

2 Enlarge shape B by scale factor −0.5, centre (1, 2)

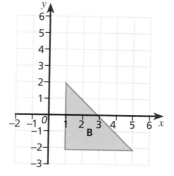

3 Describe fully the single transformation that maps shape R onto shape S.

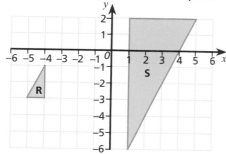

4 Describe fully the single transformation that maps shape U onto shape T.

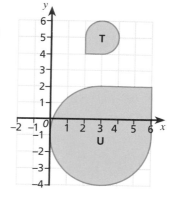

Further

1 Enlarge the trapezium shown on the grid by scale factor $-\frac{3}{2}$, centre (−2, −1)   (3 marks)

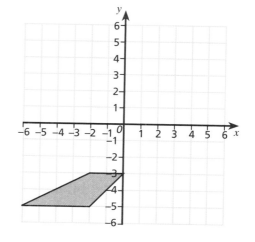

2 Shape P has been transformed to shape Q. Heidi describes the single transformation of P to Q as a rotation 180° about (−7, 4)

Give another possible single transformation of P to Q.   (2 marks)

4.2 Invariance

Foundations

Write the equation of each straight line.

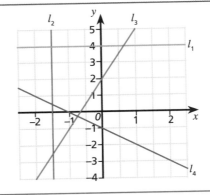

Facts

When a shape undergoes a transformation, the points of that shape usually change position. However, some points may remain in the same position. These are known as **invariant** points.

Under a rotation, if the centre of rotation lies on the shape, then this point will be invariant.

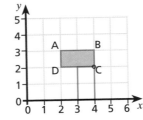

Vertex C is invariant when the rectangle is rotated 90° anticlockwise about C.

When considering a reflection, an invariant point must lie on the line of reflection.

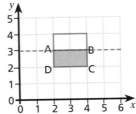

Line segment AB and vertices A and B of the rectangle are invariant when the rectangle is reflected in the line $y = 3$

Focus

Example
State the invariant line(s) or point(s) of triangle ABC if it is:

a) rotated 180° about (4, 2)

b) enlarged by scale factor 2, centre (4, 3)

c) reflected in the line $y = 2$

d) reflected in the line $y = x$

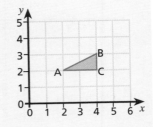

a) 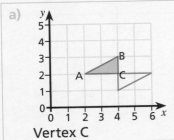 Vertex C	Vertex C is invariant as it is the centre of rotation.
b) Vertex B	Vertex B is invariant as it is the centre of the enlargement.

c)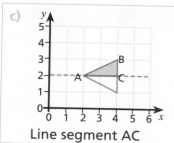
Line segment AC

Vertices A and C are invariant as they lie on the line of reflection. Line segment AC is an invariant line.

d)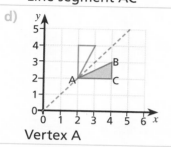
Vertex A

Vertex A is invariant as it lies on the line of reflection.

Fluency

1 State the invariant point(s) of the parallelogram ABCD if it is:

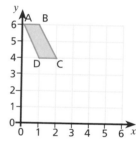

a) enlarged by scale factor 3, centre (0, 6)

b) rotated 90° clockwise about (2, 4)

c) reflected in the line $x = 1$

d) reflected in the line $x + y = 6$

2 Square PQRS with vertices P(2, 2), Q(6, 2), R(2, 6) and S(6, 6) is reflected in the line $y = x$

a) State which vertices are invariant.

b) Find the equation of the line of reflection such that Q and R are invariant.

Further

1 Parallelogram EFGH has vertices E(1, 1), F(2, 4), G(4, 5) and H(3, 2)

Describe fully a single transformation on EFGH where there is:

a) one invariant vertex   (2 marks)

b) an invariant side   (2 marks)

c) a pair of opposite vertices which are invariant   (2 marks)

2 Rectangle A is translated and labelled B, as shown.

Mo says there is one invariant vertex.

Explain why Mo is wrong.   (1 mark)

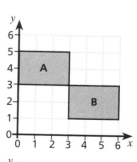

3 Beca conjectures, "It is impossible for a shape to have a point of invariance after a translation."

Use a counter-example to disprove Beca's conjecture.   (1 mark)

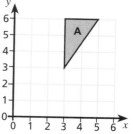

4 Work out the coordinates of the invariant point on triangle A when it is rotated 180°, centre (4, 3) and then reflected in the line $y = x$, and then enlarged by scale factor $\frac{1}{2}$, centre (3, 1)   (4 marks)

Foundations

Calculate the sizes of the angles marked with letters.

a)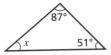

b)

c)

d)

Facts

Here are the first four circle theorems. The others are covered in the next unit.

1	2	3	4
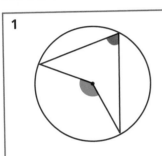	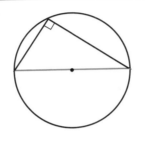	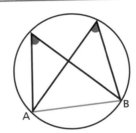	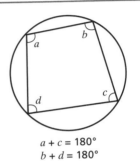 $a + c = 180°$ $b + d = 180°$
The angle at the centre is twice the angle at the circumference.	The angle in a semi-circle is a right angle.	Angles in the same segment are equal.	Opposite angles in a cyclic quadrilateral have a sum of 180°

A **segment** is an area formed by a chord and an arc. In diagram 3, the chord AB subtends the two angles labelled as equal.

A quadrilateral is **cyclic** if all four vertices touch the circumference of the circle.

Focus

Example

Work out the sizes of angles x and y. Give reasons for your answers.

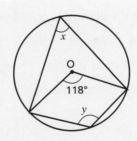

$118° = 2x$ $x = 59°$ The angle at the centre is twice the angle at the circumference.	The angle at the centre is twice the angle x. $2x = 118°$ Divide both sides of the equation by 2 to find the value of x. Give the full mathematical reason.
$180° - 59° = 121°$ $y = 121°$ Opposite angles in a cyclic quadrilateral have a sum of 180°	Angle y is opposite angle x, which we now know is 59° Opposite angles in a cyclic quadrilateral have a sum of 180°, so $y + 59° = 180°$ Subtract 59 from both sides to get $y = 121°$

Fluency

① Calculate the size of each angle marked with a letter.

a)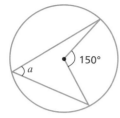

b)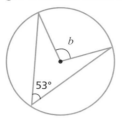

② Calculate the size of each angle marked with a letter.

a)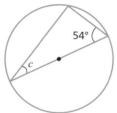

b)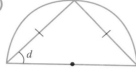

c)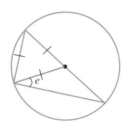

③ Calculate the size of each angle marked with a letter.

a)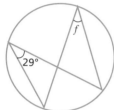

b)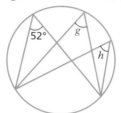

④ Calculate the size of each angle marked with a letter.

a)

b)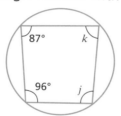

c)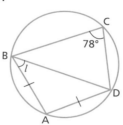

Further

① Calculate the size of angle OZY. (3 marks)

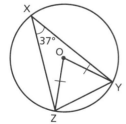

② Work out the size of the angle marked *x*. (3 marks)

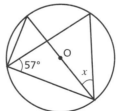

③ Work out the size of angle BOC. (2 marks)

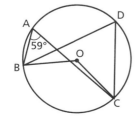

④ Work out the values of *m* and of *q*. (3 marks)

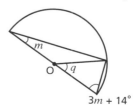

Foundations

Calculate the sizes of the angles marked with letters.

a)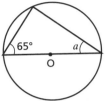

b)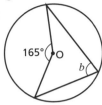

c)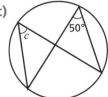

d)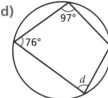

Facts

Here are the remaining circle theorems.

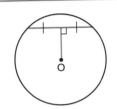		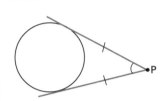	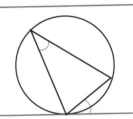
A perpendicular from the centre to a chord bisects the chord.	The angle between a tangent and a radius is a right angle.	Two tangents to a circle from the same point are equal in length.	The angle between a chord and a tangent is equal to the angle at the circumference in the alternate segment. This is known as the **alternate segment theorem**.

A **tangent** is a straight line segment touching the circumference of a circle at exactly one point.

A **chord** is a line segment which joins two points on the circumference of a circle, and splits the circle into two **segments**.

Focus

Example
Work out the size of angle MLN.

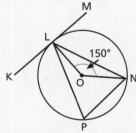

150 = 2 × ∠LPN as the angle at the centre is twice the angle at the circumference.	∠LON is at the centre and is twice ∠LPN.
	2 × ∠LPN = 150°
	Divide both sides of the equation by 2 to find ∠LPN.
75° = ∠LPN	
∠MLN = ∠LPN = 75°	∠MLN is the angle between a tangent and the chord, which creates the segment ∠LPN is in. This is the alternate segment theorem, therefore
Alternate segment theorem	∠LPN = ∠MLN

Fluency

1 M is the midpoint of the chord AC in the circle with centre O.

Calculate the size of angle BAC.

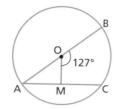

2 CD is a tangent to the circle, centre O.

Find the size of angle BDC.

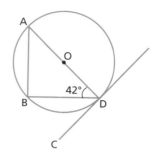

3 DE and DF are tangents to the circle at E and F. O is the centre of the circle.

Calculate the size of angle OEF.

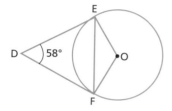

4 Calculate the sizes of angles x and y.

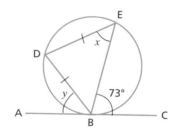

Further

1 A and B are points on the circumference of a circle, centre O.

DCE is a tangent to the circle. Angle ACD = 76°

a) Work out the size of angle ACO. Give reasons for each stage of your working. (2 marks)

b) Work out the size of angle ABC. Give reasons for each stage of your working. (2 marks)

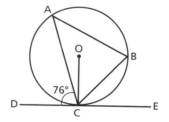

2 A, B, C and D are points on the circumference of a circle, centre O. Angle AOC = x

Work out the size of angle ABC in terms of x. (2 marks)

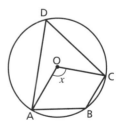

3 A, B, C and D are points on the circumference of a circle, centre O.

Prove that the triangles ABD and ACD are congruent. (3 marks)

> See unit 4.5 for details about congruence.

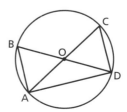

Foundations

The two triangles are congruent.

a) Which side of triangle ABC corresponds to XY?

b) Which side is between angle ACB and angle ABC?

c) Write down the length of side XY.

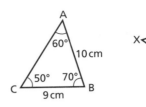

Facts

Congruent shapes are exactly the same shape and size. There are four sets of conditions which determine if two triangles are congruent.

SAS: two sides and the included angle are the same	**ASA:** two angles and the included side are the same
 	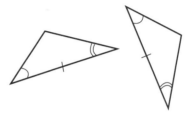
SSS: three sides are the same	**RHS:** right-angled triangles with both a hypotenuse and one other side that are equal
	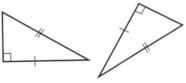

Focus

Example 1

ABCD is a kite.

a) Explain why triangles DAB and DCB are not congruent.

b) Explain why triangles ADC and CBA are congruent.

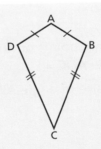

a) 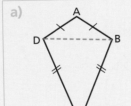	The triangle DAB and DCB are two different isosceles triangles.	Show the two triangles and explain clearly why they are not congruent.
	The two triangles do not have any of the same angles and they only share one common side, DB.	
	Therefore the triangles are not congruent.	

b)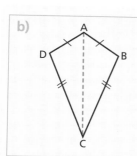

Side AB = AD, side BC = DC and the triangles share a common side, AC.

The triangles are congruent as they satisfy the condition side, side, side (SSS).

Identify the equal sides and give the reason why the triangles are congruent.

Example 2

Prove that triangles CDE and ACB are congruent.

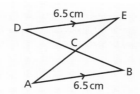

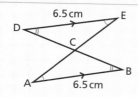

∠DEC = ∠BAC and ∠ABC = ∠CDE as alternate angles in parallel lines are equal.	Use your knowledge of parallel line angles.
AB = DE	Use the given information.
ABC and CDE are congruent (ASA)	State the condition you have used to show congruence.

Fluency

1 Explain why triangles ABC and XYZ are congruent.

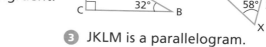

Hint: Use Pythagoras' theorem.

2 ABCD is a rhombus.

Show that triangles ABC and ADC are congruent.

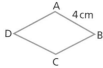

3 JKLM is a parallelogram.

Prove that triangle JKM is congruent to KLM.

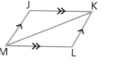

4 PQRS is a square. The diagonal lines pass through the centre of the square.

Show that triangle PTQ is congruent to STR.

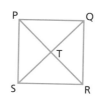

Further

1 E and F are points on a circle with centre O.

GE and GF are tangents to the circle.

Prove that the triangles GOE and GOF are congruent.   (3 marks)

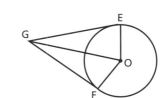

2 ACF is a triangle.

ABDE is a parallelogram.

B is the midpoint of AC.

D is the midpoint of FC.

E is the midpoint of AF.

Prove that EDF and BCD are congruent triangles.   (4 marks)

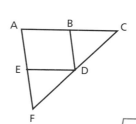

Foundations

1 Show that the rectangles are similar.

10 cm

3.75 cm

4 cm

1.5 cm

2 Work out the surface area and volume of the cuboid.

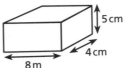

5 cm

4 cm

8 m

Facts

In **similar shapes**, the lengths of the corresponding sides are in the same ratio.

You work out the scale factor of enlargement of similar shapes for **length**, **area** and **volume** by comparing corresponding sides, areas or volumes.

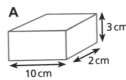

A

3 cm

2 cm

10 cm

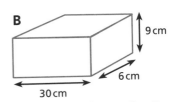

B

9 cm

6 cm

30 cm

The linear scale factor can be found by comparing any of the corresponding sides, for example $9 \div 3 = 3$

The volume of A is $60\,cm^3$ and the volume of B is $1620\,cm^3$, so the volume scale factor is found by $1620 \div 60 = 27$. Notice that the volume scale factor is the cube of the scale factor of the lengths.

In general, the scale factor for **areas** is the scale factor of the lengths squared.

In general, the scale factor for **volumes** is the scale factor of the lengths cubed.

Focus

Example 1

A 3-D printer prints two similar cuboids.

a) The surface area of cuboid A is $276\,cm^2$
Work out the surface area of cuboid B.

b) The volume of cuboid B is $17\,920\,cm^3$
Work out the volume of cuboid A.

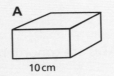

A

10 cm

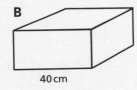

B

40 cm

a) Length scale factor $= 40 \div 10 = 4$ Area scale factor $= 4^2 = 16$ $276 \times 16 = 4416\,cm^2$	Find the length scale factor using the corresponding sides 10 cm and 40 cm. Square this to find the area scale factor. Multiply the known surface area of cuboid A by 16 to find the surface area of B.
b) Volume scale factor $= 4^3 = 64$ $17\,920 \div 64 = 280\,cm^3$	Find the volume scale factor by cubing the length scale factor. Divide the known volume of cuboid B by 64 to find the volume of A. You need to divide as the volume of cuboid A must be less than the volume of B.

Example 2

X and Y are similar shapes.

Calculate the surface area of shape Y to 3 significant figures.

Volume $2000\,mm^3$
Surface area $905\,mm^2$

X

Y

Volume $250\,mm^3$

Volume scale factor = 2000 ÷ 250 = 8	Find the volume scale factor by dividing the volume of X by the volume of Y.
Length scale factor = $\sqrt[3]{8}$ = 2	Find the scale factor of the lengths by taking the cube root of the volume scale factor.
Area scale factor = 2^2 = 4	Calculate the area scale factor by squaring the scale factor of the lengths.
905 ÷ 4 = 226.25 ≈ 226 mm²	Then find the surface area of Y by dividing the surface area of X by 4

Fluency

1 Complete the table.

Linear scale factor	Area scale factor	Volume scale factor
3		
	25	
		64
		1000
	30.25	

2 Jakub and Rosie are working out the linear scale factor of enlargement from shape A to B.

Jakub says the linear scale factor from A to B is 8

Rosie says the linear scale factor from A to B is $\frac{1}{8}$

a) Explain who is correct and why.

b) Calculate the area scale factor from shape B to A.

A 12 m B 1.5 m

3 A hexagonal prism has been enlarged, as shown.

a) What is the length scale factor?

b) What is the area scale factor?

c) What is the volume scale factor?

d) Use the volume scale factor to find the volume of the larger prism.

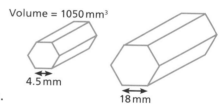

Volume = 1050 mm³
4.5 mm
18 mm

Further

1 A rectangle has been enlarged. The area scale factor of enlargement of the rectangle is 6.25

The width of the enlarged rectangle is 5 cm. What is the width of the original rectangle? (2 marks)

2 Two bottles are mathematically similar.

Their capacities are shown.

Work out the value of x. (2 marks)

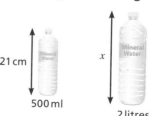

21 cm 500 ml x 2 litres

3 M and N are two geometrically similar, solid shapes.

The total surface area of shape M is 1800 mm²

The total surface area of shape N is 11 250 mm²

The volume of shape N is 3000 mm³

Calculate the volume of shape M. (3 marks)

4 Cylinder A has a surface area of 340 cm² and a volume of 500 cm³

Cylinder B has a surface area of 1632 cm² and a volume of 2400 cm³

Are these cylinders similar? Explain your answer. (3 marks)

Foundations

1 Calculate AC.

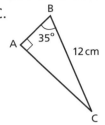

2 Calculate angle EDF.

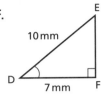

Facts

The rules and theorems that are used to solve problems in 2-D shapes can also be used for right-angled triangles in 3-D shapes.

Pythagoras' theorem: $a^2 + b^2 = \text{hypotenuse}^2$

Trigonometry: $\sin \theta = \dfrac{\text{opp}}{\text{hyp}}$ $\cos \theta = \dfrac{\text{adj}}{\text{hyp}}$ $\tan \theta = \dfrac{\text{opp}}{\text{adj}}$

You can identify right-angled triangles in 3-D shapes.

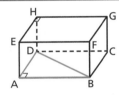	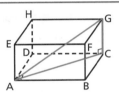
Triangles ADB, BDC, EFH and GHF are congruent right-angled triangles.	Triangles CAG, CAE, BDF and HFD are congruent right-angled triangles.

Focus

Example

ABCDEFGH is a cuboid.

a) Calculate the length AG, giving your answer to 3 significant figures.

b) Calculate the angle CAG to 1 decimal place.

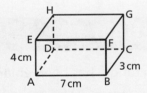

a) $AC = \sqrt{7^2 + 3^2}$ $AC = \sqrt{58}$ cm	Work out the diagonal AC using Pythagoras' theorem.
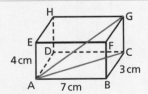 $AC^2 + CG^2 = AG^2$ $58 + 4^2 = AG^2$ $AG = \sqrt{74}$ cm $AG = 8.60$ cm (3 s.f.)	Using the theorem again in triangle ACG, work out the length AG using the length AC; you know $AC^2 = 58$ cm

b)

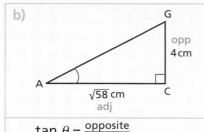

	From the diagram of the cuboid, you can see the right-angled triangle ACG. You may find it useful to draw this separately. Label the sides so you know which trigonometric ratio to use.
$\tan \theta = \frac{\text{opposite}}{\text{adjacent}}$	As you know the opposite side and the adjacent side, use the tangent ratio to work out angle CAG.
$\tan \theta = \frac{4}{\sqrt{58}}$ $\theta = \tan^{-1}\left(\frac{4}{\sqrt{58}}\right)$	You know that GC = 4 cm and AC = $\sqrt{58}$ cm from part a) of the question. It is important to use the exact value, not the rounded value.
Angle CAG = 27.7° (1 d.p.)	As you also know the length of AG from part a), you could use any of the three trigonometric ratios and get the same answer.

Fluency

1 ABCDEFGH is a cuboid.

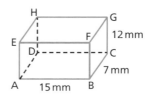

Which of the following are right-angled triangles?

ADB   GED   HBD   BDF   CGA   GBE

2 Using cuboid ABCDEFGH from question 1:
   a) calculate the exact length of BD
   b) calculate the length BH, giving your answer to 3 significant figures
   c) calculate angle DHB, giving your answer to 1 decimal place

3 ABCDEFGH is a cube.

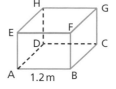

   a) Calculate the length CE. Give your answer to 3 significant figures.
   b) Calculate the angle FHB. Round your answer to the nearest integer.

4 Calculate the length of the longest diagonal in a cuboid that has a width of 10 cm, a height of 5 cm and a depth of 8 cm.

Further

1 The diagram shows a triangular prism.

The angle RQU is 30°

Calculate the size of the angle between SQ and QT.
Give your answer correct to 1 decimal place.   (4 marks)

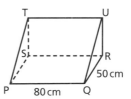

2 The diagram shows a square-based pyramid.

VY is 9 cm.

Angle ZYW is 75°

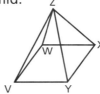

Calculate the volume of the pyramid. Give your answer to 3 significant figures.   (4 marks)

Volume of a pyramid = $\frac{1}{3}$ × base area × height

4.8 Sine rule

Foundations

Solve the equations.

a) $\sin x = 0.7$

b) $\sin 40 = \dfrac{y}{10.3}$

c) $\dfrac{a}{\sin 63} = \dfrac{7}{\sin 45}$

Facts

The **sine rule** helps you to find angles and sides in triangles that are not right-angled.

The vertices can be labelled A, B and C and these can be used to describe the angles. The sides opposite each vertex are labelled a, b and c.

Angle A is directly opposite side a.

The sine rule states:

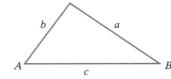

$$\frac{a}{\sin A} = \frac{b}{\sin B} = \frac{c}{\sin C} \quad \text{or} \quad \frac{\sin A}{a} = \frac{\sin B}{b} = \frac{\sin C}{c}$$

To use the sine rule, you need an angle and the side opposite it and one other angle or side.

You use the form $\dfrac{a}{\sin A} = \dfrac{b}{\sin B} = \dfrac{c}{\sin C}$ when working out a side and the form $\dfrac{\sin A}{a} = \dfrac{\sin B}{b} = \dfrac{\sin C}{c}$ when working out an angle. You only need to use two of the fractions from the formula in any one part of a question. See the example below.

Focus

Example

a) Calculate the length of CB.

Give your answer to 3 significant figures.

b) Work out the acute angle labelled y.

Give your answer to the nearest integer.

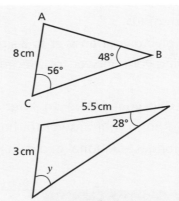

a) $\dfrac{a}{\sin A} = \dfrac{b}{\sin B}$ Angle BAC = 180 − 56 − 48 = 76° 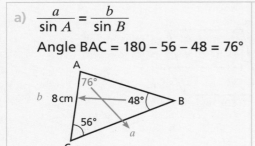	Since you have two angles and a length opposite, you can use the sine rule to find the missing length CB. CB is opposite angle BAC, so you need to start by working this out.
$\dfrac{CB}{\sin 76} = \dfrac{8}{\sin 48}$	Substitute the values into the formula. You only need to use two of the three fractions from the formula.
$CB = \dfrac{8}{\sin 48} \times \sin 76 = 10.4$ cm	Rearrange the equation and make sure your calculator is in degrees mode.

b) $\dfrac{\sin A}{a} = \dfrac{\sin B}{b}$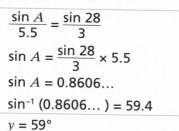

Since you are finding an angle, you can use the formula written in this format.

Label the triangle and substitute the values into the formula.

$\dfrac{\sin A}{5.5} = \dfrac{\sin 28}{3}$ $\sin A = \dfrac{\sin 28}{3} \times 5.5$ $\sin A = 0.8606\ldots$ $\sin^{-1}(0.8606\ldots) = 59.4$	Rearrange the equation and use the inverse sine function to find the value of y.
$y = 59°$	Write your answer to the nearest integer.

Fluency

1 Work out the lengths labelled x and y in the triangles. Give your answers to 3 significant figures.

a)
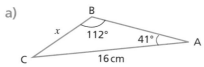

b)
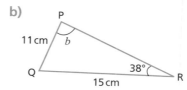

2 Work out the angles labelled a and b in the triangles. Give your answers to 3 significant figures.

a)
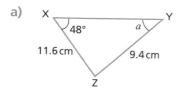

b)
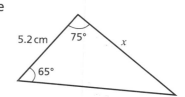

3 In triangle ABC, BC = 5 cm, angle ABC = 126° and angle BAC = 28°

Work out the length of AC.

4 In triangle PQR, PQ = 79 mm, QR = 70 mm and angle PRQ = 99°

Work out the size of angle RPQ.

Further

1 Rob thinks it is impossible to find the length marked x in this triangle as you are not given the length of a side opposite a known angle.

a) Explain why Rob is wrong. (1 mark)

b) Calculate the length marked x, giving your answer correct to 1 decimal place. (2 marks)

2 Prove that there is no triangle ABC where angle BAC = 58°, BC = 6 cm and AC = 9 cm (2 marks)

3 Show that there are two possible triangles where angle BAC = 10°, BC = 6 cm and AC = 12 cm (3 marks)

Foundations

Solve the equations.

a) $a^2 = 74.32$ b) $90\cos A = 70$

Facts

The **cosine rule** is another rule that helps you find angles and sides in triangles that are not right-angled.

The cosine rule states:

$$a^2 = b^2 + c^2 - 2bc\cos A$$

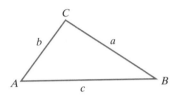

A is the **included angle** which is the angle between the two given sides.

To use the cosine rule, you need all three sides and one angle, or two sides and the angle between them.
Remember that to use the sine rule, you need an angle and the side opposite it and one other angle or side. You will often need to decide which rule to use when solving problems involving triangles that are not right-angled.

Focus

Example

a) Work out the length of DY.
Give your answer to 1 decimal place.

b) Calculate the size of angle TRS.
Give your answer to 2 decimal places.

a) $a^2 = b^2 + c^2 - 2bc\cos A$	Since you have two lengths and the included angle, you can use the cosine rule to find the required length.
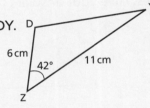	Label the triangle and substitute the values into the formula.
$a^2 = 6^2 + 11^2 - 2 \times 6 \times 11\cos 42$ $a^2 = 58.9048...$ $a = \sqrt{58.9048...}$ DY = 7.67 cm	This gives the value of a^2, so you need to find the square root.
b) 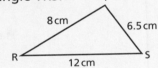	Since you have three lengths, you can use the cosine rule to find the required angle. Label the triangle and substitute the values that you know into the formula.

$a^2 = b^2 + c^2 - 2bc\cos A$
$6.5^2 = 8^2 + 12^2 - 2 \times 8 \times 12 \times \cos A$
$42.25 = 208 - 192\cos A$
+ 192 cos$A$ + 192 cos$A$
$192\cos A + 42.25 = 208$
− 42.25   − 42.25
$192\cos A = 165.75$
÷ 192   ÷ 192
$\cos x = \frac{221}{256}$
$\cos^{-1}\left(\frac{221}{256}\right) = 30.313$
Angle TRS = 30.3°

Rearrange the equation and use the inverse cosine function to find the value of the angle.

Depending on your calculator, you may get a fraction like this or a decimal equivalent 0.863 281 25...

Fluency

1 Work out the length of AB, giving your answer to 3 significant figures.

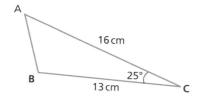

2 Work out the size of angle BAC, giving your answer to the nearest degree.

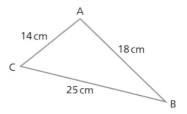

3 Work out the lengths labelled x and y in the triangles.

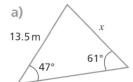

4 Work out the angles labelled g and h in the triangles.

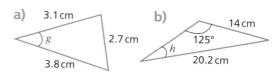

5 EFG is an isosceles triangle.

Work out the length of FG.

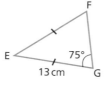

6 In triangle QRS, angle QRS is 68°
Side QR is 7.3 cm and side RS is 45 mm.

Find the perimeter of the triangle.

Further

1 Calculate the size of angle WXY.
Give your answer to the nearest integer.   (4 marks)

2 The diagram shows sector XOY.

XY is a chord of length 95 mm.

Calculate the size of angle XOY.
Give your answer to 1 decimal place.   (3 marks)

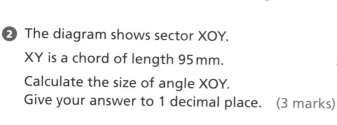

3 Calculate the value of y, giving your answer in surd form.   (4 marks)

4.10 Area of a general triangle

Foundations

1 Solve to find the value of a.

$5 = \frac{1}{2}a \times 4\sin(22)$

2 Solve to find the value of θ.

$3 = \frac{1}{2} \times 8 \times \sin\theta$

Facts

The area of any triangle can be found using the formula $\text{Area} = \frac{1}{2}ab\sin C$

You can think of this as the area of a triangle being equal to half the product of two of the sides and the sine of the **included** angle (the angle between two given sides).

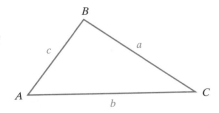

Focus

Example 1

Calculate the area of the triangle.
Give your answer to 3 significant figures.

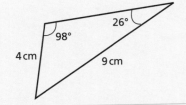

$\text{Area} = \frac{1}{2}ab\sin C$	Write down the formula.
	Label the triangle with a, b and C. Remember C needs to be the included angle, so the angle between 4 cm and 9 cm. It doesn't matter which side is a and which is b.
$180° - 98° - 26° = 56°$	The included angle is not given so you need to work it out using the sum of the angles in a triangle.
$\text{Area} = \frac{1}{2} \times 9 \times 4 \times \sin 56$	Substitute the values into the formula.
$= 14.9\,\text{cm}^2$	Give your answer to 3 significant figures.

Example 2

The area of the triangle is $2.4\,\text{m}^2$

Calculate the size of angle θ. Give your answer to 1 decimal place.

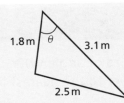

$\text{Area} = \frac{1}{2}ab\sin C$	Start by writing the formula and substitute in what you know.
$2.4 = \frac{1}{2} \times 1.8 \times 3.1\sin\theta$	θ is between the sides of 1.8 m and 3.1 m, so you need to use those for your lengths of a and b.
$2.4 = 2.79\sin\theta$	Simplify the equation.
$\frac{2.4}{2.79} = \sin\theta$	Rearrange.
$\theta = \sin^{-1}\left(\frac{2.4}{2.79}\right)$	Use the inverse function to find the value of θ.
$\theta = 59.3°$	

Fluency

1 Work out the areas of the triangles, giving your answers to 3 significant figures.

a)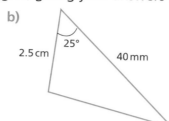

b)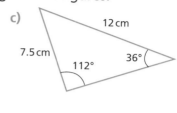

c)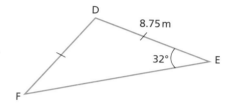

2 Find the area of DEF. Give your answer to 3 significant figures.

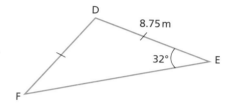

3 The area of each triangle is 50 cm²

Work out the values of x and θ, giving your answers to the nearest integer.

a)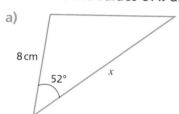

b)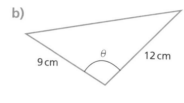

4 Here is some information about triangle ABC.

AB = 15 cm, BC = 12 cm and AC = 17 cm

Angle BAC = 43°

Calculate the area of triangle ABC, giving your answer to 2 decimal places.

Further

1 The area of this triangle is 30 cm²

Calculate the length of x.   (3 marks)

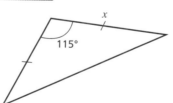

2 The diagram shows sector EOF.

EF is a chord.

Calculate the area of the shaded region.
Give your answer to 3 significant figures.   (4 marks)

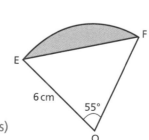

Foundations

1 Write the vector shown as a column vector.

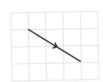

2 Write $\overrightarrow{XZ}$ in terms of **p** and **q**.

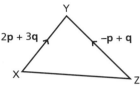

Facts

A **vector** has both magnitude (size) and direction.

Vectors can be written using the notation $\overrightarrow{XY}$ to show the start and end points, in this case 'the vector from X to Y'.

Vectors can also be expressed using single letters, such as **a**, and this is useful for comparing them. For example, 3**a** is the vector in the same direction as **a** but three times as long. −**a** is the same length as **a** but in the opposite direction.

Vectors that are multiples of each other are **parallel**. For example, 4**p** + 6**q** is parallel to 2**p** + 3**q** as

4**p** + 6**q** = 2(2**p** + 3**q**)

Three or more points are **collinear** if they all lie on the same straight line. If the vectors $\overrightarrow{XY}$ and $\overrightarrow{XZ}$ are parallel, you know the points X, Y and Z are collinear because both vectors go through X.

Focus

Example 1
OXY is a triangle.
M is the midpoint of OX.
N is the midpoint of OY.
$\overrightarrow{OX} = \mathbf{x}$ and $\overrightarrow{OY} = \mathbf{y}$
Show that MN is parallel to XY.

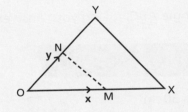

$\overrightarrow{XY} = \overrightarrow{XO} + \overrightarrow{OY} = -\mathbf{x} + \mathbf{y}$ $\overrightarrow{MN} = \overrightarrow{MO} + \overrightarrow{ON}$ $\overrightarrow{MN} = -\frac{1}{2}\mathbf{x} + \frac{1}{2}\mathbf{y} = \frac{1}{2}(-\mathbf{x} + \mathbf{y})$	Work out the vectors $\overrightarrow{XY}$ and $\overrightarrow{MN}$ in terms of **x** and **y**.
$\overrightarrow{XY}$ is a multiple of $\overrightarrow{MN}$ $-\mathbf{x} + \mathbf{y} = 2 \times \frac{1}{2}(-\mathbf{x} + \mathbf{y})$ XY and MN are parallel.	To show that vectors are parallel, you need to show that one vector is a multiple of another.

Example 2
AY : YB = 1 : 2
Work out $\overrightarrow{AY}$ in terms of **p** and **q**.

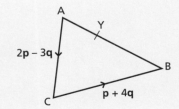

$\overrightarrow{AB} = \overrightarrow{AC} + \overrightarrow{CB}$

$\overrightarrow{AB} = 2p - 3q + p + 4q = 3p + q$

	Start by calculating the vector AB in terms of **p** and **q**.
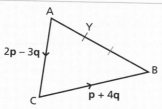	As the ratio of AY : YB is 1 : 2, you can separate AB into three equal parts. You can now see that AY is one-third of the length of AB.

$\overrightarrow{AY} = \frac{1}{3}\overrightarrow{AB} = \frac{1}{3}(3p + q) = p + \frac{1}{3}q$

Fluency

1 ABCD is a square.

The diagonals AC and BD intersect at N.

$\overrightarrow{AB} = a$ and $\overrightarrow{AD} = b$

Write the following vectors in terms of **a** and **b**.

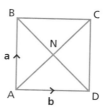

a) $\overrightarrow{DA}$ b) $\overrightarrow{BC}$ c) $\overrightarrow{NA}$ d) $\overrightarrow{DB}$ e) $\overrightarrow{DN}$ f) $\overrightarrow{CN}$

2 OXYZ is a rhombus.

$\overrightarrow{OX} = x$ and $\overrightarrow{OZ} = z$

Q lies on OY such that OQ : QY = 1 : 4

Work out the vector in terms of **x** and **z** that represents:

a) $\overrightarrow{XY}$ b) $\overrightarrow{OY}$ c) $\overrightarrow{OQ}$ d) $\overrightarrow{YQ}$

3 $\overrightarrow{OA} = 3a$ and $\overrightarrow{OB} = 5b$

X is a point on AB such that AX : XB = 2 : 3

$\overrightarrow{OX} = k(9a + 10b)$

Find the value of k.

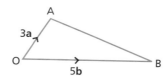

Further

1 ORST is a parallelogram.

$\overrightarrow{OR} = r$ and $\overrightarrow{RS} = s$

a) Express in terms of **r** and **s** these vectors.

   i) $\overrightarrow{OS}$ ii) $\overrightarrow{OT}$ iii) $\overrightarrow{RT}$ (3 marks)

b) N is the point on ST extended such that ST : TN = 1 : 2

   P is the point on OT such that OP = $\frac{1}{3}$ OT

   Show that R, P and N all lie on the same straight line.   (2 marks)

2 ABCDEF is a regular hexagon with centre O.

$\overrightarrow{OA} = a$ and $\overrightarrow{OF} = b$

M is the midpoint of FE.

X is the point on AF extended such that AF : FX = 3 : 2

Prove that C, M and X are collinear.   (5 marks)

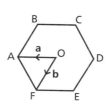

Facts

Probability measures the chance of something happening, ranging from 0 (impossible) to 1 (certain). Probabilities are written as fractions, decimals or percentages. If all the possible outcomes of an event are equally likely, then:

$$P(\text{outcome}) = \frac{\text{Number of ways the outcome could happen}}{\text{Total number of outcomes}}$$

where P(outcome) is used as a short way of saying 'the probability of the outcome'.

As the sum of all possible probabilities is 1, then P(outcome not happening) = 1 − P(outcome happening)

A **sample space diagram** is a table used to represent all possible outcomes of an event. For example, this diagram shows the possible outcomes when throwing two fair dice and finding the total. From the diagram you can see that $P(4) = \frac{3}{36}$, which you can simplify to $\frac{1}{12}$

+	1	2	3	4	5	6
1	2	3	4	5	6	7
2	3	4	5	6	7	8
3	4	5	6	7	8	9
4	5	6	7	8	9	10
5	6	7	8	9	10	11
6	7	8	9	10	11	12

You can use probability to work out the **expected number** of times an outcome will happen. For example, if two dice are thrown 300 times, you would expect a total of 4 about $\frac{1}{12} \times 300 = 25$ times

If you don't know the probability of an outcome, you can perform an experiment and use the **relative frequency** of the outcome $\left(\dfrac{\text{Number of times the outcome occurs}}{\text{Total number of trials}}\right)$ as an estimate. A large number of trials gives greater accuracy.

Two events, A and B, are **independent** if the outcome of one does not affect the outcome of the other. If A and B are independent, then **P(A and B) = P(A) × P(B)**. For example, the probability of throwing a 6 on a fair dice and flipping a head on a fair coin is $\frac{1}{6} \times \frac{1}{2} = \frac{1}{12}$

You can use **tree diagrams** to show the probabilities of independent events. For example, consider a bag that contains 5 red counters and 4 blue counters. If a counter is chosen at random, replaced and then another counter is chosen, a tree diagram can show this as:

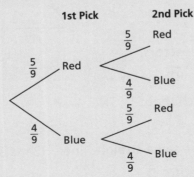

P(both counters are red) = $\frac{5}{9} \times \frac{5}{9} = \frac{25}{81}$

P(exactly one counter is red) = P(R, B) + P(B, R)

$$= \left(\frac{5}{9} \times \frac{4}{9}\right) + \left(\frac{4}{9} \times \frac{5}{9}\right) = \frac{40}{81}$$

Practice

1. Use the sample space diagram on page 98 for the total score when two dice are thrown to find the probability that the total is:

   a) 7   b) even   c) a multiple of 3

2. The table shows the probabilities that a spinner lands on different colours.

Colour	Red	Green	Yellow	Blue	Purple
Probability	0.36	0.22	0.22		0.04

   Work out the probability that the spinner:

   a) lands on blue   b) does not land on yellow

3. A bag contains red, white and blue counters.

   The probability of selecting a red counter is $\frac{3}{7}$

   There are 14 white counters and an equal number of red and blue counters in the bag.

   How many counters are in the bag in total?

4. a) The probability that a biased coin lands on heads is 0.4

      The coin is thrown 200 times. How many times would you expect it to land on tails?

   b) Another coin is thrown 200 times and lands on heads 108 times.

      Do you think the coin is fair? Explain your answer.

5. There are 120 students in Years 10 and 11. They all study one of French, Spanish or German.

   a) Complete the two-way table.

	French	Spanish	German	Total
Year 10				72
Year 11	28		11	
Total		45	32	

   b) A student is selected at random.

      i)   Find the probability that the student studies Spanish.

      ii) Find the probability that the student is in Year 10 and studies German.

      iii) Given that the student is in Year 11, find the probability that they study Spanish.

6. A and B are independent events such that P(A) = $\frac{2}{7}$ and P(B) = $\frac{3}{5}$

   Work out the probability that: a) both A and B occur   b) neither A nor B occur

7. Jackson throws three fair dice.

   Work out the probability that they all land on 6

8. In a bag of 10 counters, 3 are red and the rest are green. One counter is selected at random, put back in the bag and then a second counter is taken.

   a) Draw a tree diagram to show the probabilities that the counters selected are red or green.

   b) Work out the probability that exactly one of the counters selected is green.

Facts

Statistical diagrams are used to represent data visually.

In a **bar chart**, the height of the bar is proportional to the frequency of the item. More than one set of data can be shown on a multiple bar chart.

In a **pie chart**, the area of the sector is proportional to the frequency.

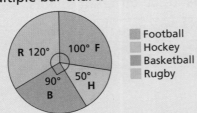

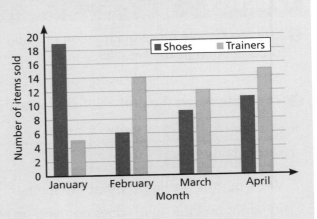

A **scatter diagram** is used to show **bivariate** data. You can see whether there is any **correlation** between the two variables.

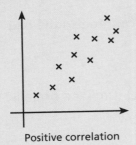

Positive correlation

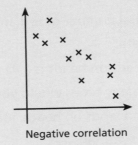

Negative correlation

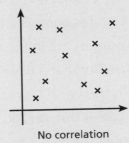

No correlation

You can use a **line of best fit** to estimate one value given another.

A line of best fit is a straight line that is drawn as close to the points as possible. Notice that the line does not need to go through the origin.

Frequency trees and **Venn diagrams** can be used to organise information.

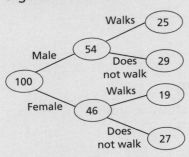

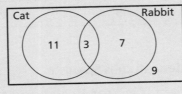

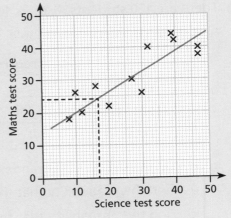

A **time series graph** shows how data changes over time.

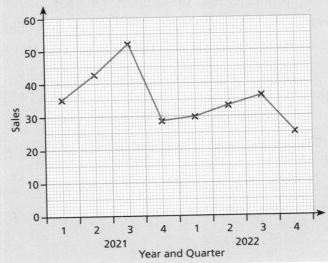

A **frequency polygon** shows the frequency of a group plotted against the **midpoint** of each group. A **cumulative frequency diagram** shows the amount of data up to given points in a distribution of data and can be used to estimate the median and quartiles of a distribution.

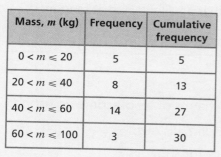

Mass, m (kg)	Frequency	Cumulative frequency
$0 < m \leqslant 20$	5	5
$20 < m \leqslant 40$	8	13
$40 < m \leqslant 60$	14	27
$60 < m \leqslant 100$	3	30

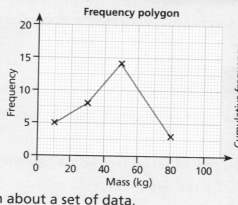

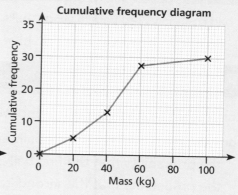

A **box plot** shows key information about a set of data.

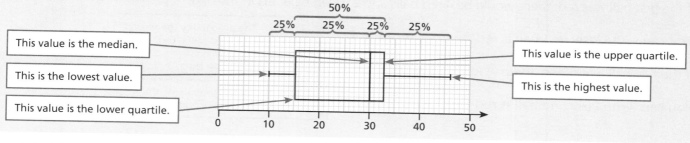

Practice

1 The table shows information about the eye colours of 120 students.

Eye colour	Blue	Brown	Green	Other
Frequency	38	64	12	6

Draw a pie chart to represent this information.

Hint: the angles in the pie chart will add up to 360°

2 There are 330 students altogether in Years 7 and 8.

They all study either French or Spanish, but not both.

110 of the 195 students who study Spanish are in Year 8.

75 students in Year 7 study French.

Complete the frequency tree.

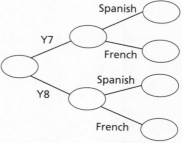

3 The table shows the amount of time that 50 people take to complete an online game.

Time, t (minutes)	$0 < t \leqslant 30$	$30 < t \leqslant 60$	$60 < t \leqslant 90$	$90 < t \leqslant 120$	$120 < t \leqslant 150$
Frequency	17	22	8	2	1

a) Draw a frequency polygon to represent this data.

b) Draw a cumulative frequency diagram to represent this data.

c) Use your cumulative frequency diagram to find the median and the interquartile range of the times taken.

d) The fastest time taken was 8 minutes and the slowest time taken was 145 minutes.

   Draw a box plot to represent the data.

5.1 Conditional probability

Foundations

A bag contains 3 red balls, 5 yellow balls and 4 blue balls. Find the probability that a ball selected at random is:

a) blue   b) green   c) blue or red   d) not red

Facts

Conditional probabilities are found when a previous outcome affects the chance of an outcome occurring.

For example, if you have 5 red balls and 2 green balls in a bag and take two balls out:

- the probability that the first ball is red, often written P(first ball is red) for short, is $\frac{5}{7}$
- the probability that the second ball is red **depends** on the colour of the first ball.

If the first ball was red, there would be 4 red balls and 2 green balls left in the bag.

You can write P(second ball is red/first ball is red) = $\frac{4}{6}$ | This is read as 'The probability the second ball is red **given** the first ball is red'.

If the first ball was green, there would be 5 red balls and 1 green ball left in the bag.

You can write P(second ball is red/first ball is green) = $\frac{5}{6}$ | This is read as 'The probability the second ball is red given the first ball is green'.

Focus

Example 1
Here are seven cards:

1   2   3   4   5   6   7

A card is chosen at random and not replaced. A second card is then taken.

a) What is the probability that the first card selected is an even number?

b) Given that the first card chosen was odd, what is the probability that the second card will be odd?

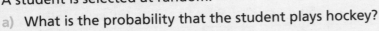

| a) P(even) = $\frac{3}{7}$ | There are seven cards, of which three are even. |
| b) P(second card is odd/first card is odd) = $\frac{3}{6} = \frac{1}{2}$ | Given that the first card was odd means there is one fewer odd card left (3) and one fewer card overall (6). |

Example 2
The Venn diagram shows the sports clubs attended by a group of students.

A student is selected at random.

a) What is the probability that the student plays hockey?

b) What is the probability that they play neither sport?

c) Given that the student plays football, what is the probability that they also play hockey?

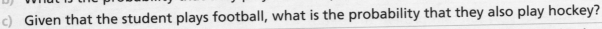

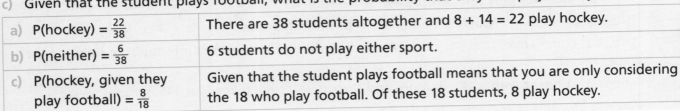

a) P(hockey) = $\frac{22}{38}$	There are 38 students altogether and 8 + 14 = 22 play hockey.
b) P(neither) = $\frac{6}{38}$	6 students do not play either sport.
c) P(hockey, given they play football) = $\frac{8}{18}$	Given that the student plays football means that you are only considering the 18 who play football. Of these 18 students, 8 play hockey.

Example 3

A box contains 3 orange sweets and 4 red sweets. Two sweets are selected at random.

a) Draw a tree diagram to show the possible outcomes.

b) Work out the probability that both sweets are orange.

a) 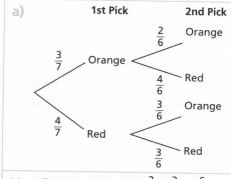	The probabilities of getting an orange or a red sweet on the second pick depend on what sweets are left in the box after the first sweet has been taken out.
b) P(both orange) = $\frac{3}{7} \times \frac{2}{6} = \frac{6}{42}$	Multiply to find the answer.

Fluency

1 Cards numbered 1 to 10 are shuffled. Two are randomly selected.

a) What is the probability that the first card shows an even number?

b) Given that the first card was an odd number, what is the probability that the second card will be even?

2 There are 40 students in Year 9. Each student studies French or Spanish. The table shows the numbers of students studying each language.

	French	Spanish
Male	12	7
Female	8	13

a) What is the probability that a student selected at random studies French?

b) Given that the student is male, what is the probability that they study Spanish?

3 A bag contains 15 sweets. Five are lemon and 10 are cola. Two sweets are taken at random.

a) Draw a tree diagram to show the information. b) Calculate the probability that both sweets are lemon.

4 Seb has 6 white socks, 4 black socks and 2 grey socks. He picks two socks at random.

a) Draw a tree diagram to show this information. | Your tree diagram will have nine branches.

b) Work out the probability that both socks will be of the same colour.

Further

1 Here are eight number cards. Two cards are selected without replacement.

0 1 1 2 3 3 3 4

What is the probability that the sum of the two cards is equal to 6? (3 marks)

2 Flo is playing chess against a computer. Games can only be won or lost. She plays two games. The probability that she wins the first game is 0.6

After the first game, the computer adjusts the level of difficulty. If Flo wins the first game, her chance of winning the second game is reduced to 0.5. But if she loses the first game, the chance of winning the second game is increased to 0.7

a) Draw a tree diagram to show this information. (2 marks)

b) Calculate the probability that Flo wins exactly one game. (2 marks)

3 A bag contains 4 blue counters and x red counters.

Two counters are removed from the bag without replacement. The probability that both counters are red is $\frac{1}{3}$

How many counters were in the bag originally? (4 marks)

Conditional probability   **103**

Foundations

If $3 < x \leqslant 10$, what integer values can x take?

Facts

In a bar chart, the bar widths are always the same and the height of each bar represents the frequency of each item.

In a **histogram**, the widths can be different and it is the **area** of the bar that represents the frequency. Histograms represent continuous data organised into groups, known as **classes**.

The heights of the bars in a histogram correspond to the **frequency densities** of the classes, which are found using the formula:

Frequency density = frequency ÷ class width

Focus

Example
The table shows information about the waiting times for some patients at a hospital.

a) Draw a histogram to show this data.

b) Estimate the number of patients that waited less than 90 minutes.

Waiting time, h (hours)	Frequency
$0 < h < 0.5$	10
$0.5 \leqslant h < 1$	15
$1 \leqslant h < 2$	8
$2 \leqslant h < 3$	8
$3 \leqslant h < 5$	2

a)

Waiting time, h (hours)	Frequency	Frequency density
$0 < h < 0.5$	10	$10 \div 0.5 = 20$
$0.5 \leqslant h < 1$	15	$15 \div 0.5 = 30$
$1 \leqslant h < 2$	8	$8 \div 1 = 8$
$2 \leqslant h < 3$	8	$8 \div 1 = 8$
$3 \leqslant h < 5$	2	$2 \div 2 = 1$

First you need to work out the height (or frequency density) of each bar.

Remember that frequency density = frequency ÷ class width

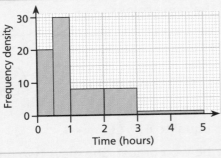

Then you need to draw your axes.
The x-axis needs to go from 0 to 5
The y-axis needs to go from 0 to 30

Now you can plot each of the bars using the table above.

b)

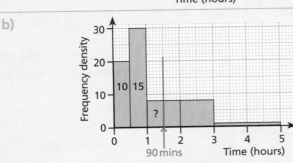

Bar 1 = 10 people   Bar 2 = 15 people
Bar 3 = 8 people $8 \div 2 = 4$ people $10 + 15 + 4 = 29$ people

Since area represents frequency, you need to find the total area to the left of the 90-minute line.

You need the total frequency of bar 1 + bar 2 + half of bar 3 (since 90 minutes is halfway through bar 3).

Fluency

1 The masses of 100 apples in an orchard are recorded in the table.

Mass, m (g)	$0 < m \leqslant 25$	$25 < m \leqslant 40$	$40 < m \leqslant 60$	$60 < m \leqslant 75$	$75 < m \leqslant 100$
Frequency	12	15	25	33	15

Draw a histogram to show this information.

2 The table shows information about the scores of some students in an assessment.

Score, s	$0 < s \leqslant 120$	$120 < s \leqslant 200$	$200 < s \leqslant 300$	$300 < s \leqslant 450$	$450 < s \leqslant 500$
Frequency	24	18	15	24	6

a) Draw a histogram to show this information.

b) Estimate the number of students who scored less than 250 marks.

> Think about the area of the bars and parts of bars that show scores $0 < s < 250$

3 This histogram shows information about the masses of some cats and kittens at a shelter.

a) Use the histogram to complete the table below.

Mass, m (kg)	$0 < m \leqslant 1.5$	$1.5 < m \leqslant 3$	$3 < m \leqslant 4$	$4 < m \leqslant 6$
Frequency				

b) Estimate the number of cats with mass greater than 3.5 kg.

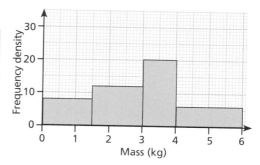

Further

1 The incomplete histogram and table below give information about the ages of customers in a supermarket.

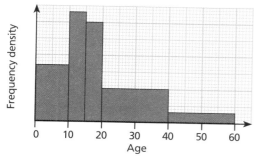

Age, a (years)	Frequency
$0 < a \leqslant 10$	34
$10 < a \leqslant 15$	33
$15 < a \leqslant 20$	
$20 < a \leqslant 40$	
$40 < a \leqslant 60$	

Use the histogram to complete the table of values.   (4 marks)

2 The table shows information about the times taken by some students to run 60 m.

Time, t (s)	$10 < t \leqslant 12$	$12 < t \leqslant 14$	$14 < t \leqslant 16$	$16 < t \leqslant 17$	$17 < t \leqslant 20$
Frequency	8	12	10		9

a) Use the table to complete the histogram.   (3 marks)

b) Use the histogram to complete the missing entry in the table.   (1 mark)

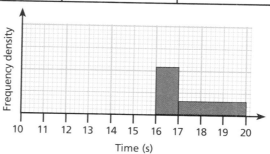

Answers

Pages 6–7
1F1 Working with number

Practice

1 a) $\frac{3}{8}$, 38%, 0.4   **b)** 0.805, 82%, $\frac{5}{6}$, $\frac{17}{20}$

2 a) $\frac{22}{15}$ or $1\frac{7}{15}$ **b)** $\frac{8}{15}$ **c)** $\frac{2}{15}$ **d)** $\frac{6}{5}$ or $1\frac{1}{5}$

3 a) $3\frac{5}{12}$ **b)** $11\frac{11}{24}$ **c)** $14\frac{2}{3}$ **d)** $3\frac{1}{3}$ **e)** $13\frac{1}{3}$ **f)** $2\frac{2}{3}$

4 500

5

Percentage	Fraction	Decimal
8%	$\frac{2}{25}$	0.08
30%	$\frac{3}{10}$	0.3
3%	$\frac{3}{100}$	0.03
2.5%	$\frac{1}{40}$	0.025
5.5%	$\frac{11}{200}$	0.055

6 a) 15 kg   **b)** 240 g   **c)** 45 m

    d) £9000   **e)** 96 cm   **f)** £280

7 a) 65.7 kg   **b)** £232.50   **c)** 102 ml   **d)** £2520

    e) £384   **f)** 0.36 kg   **g)** £1029.60 **h)** 16.8536 km

8 8%

9 a) i) £30 510   **ii)** £31 028.67   **iii)** £31 556.16

    b) £2638.19

10 × 1.3 followed by × 0.7 is equivalent to × 0.91

     91% of the original number

Pages 8–9
1.1 Estimating powers and roots

Foundations

1 a) 16   **b)** 49   **c)** 64   **d)** 81   **e)** 121

    f) 144   **g)** 8   **h)** 125   **i)** 216

2 a) 5   **b)** 10   **c)** 14   **d)** 3   **e)** 4

Fluency

1 a) $2.3^2 \approx 5$ **b)** $8.6^2 \approx 74$

    c) $5.5^2 \approx 30$ **d)** $2.3^3 \approx 12$

2 a) $\sqrt{18} \approx 4.2$ **b)** $\sqrt{92} \approx 9.6$

    c) $\sqrt{130} \approx 11.4$ **d)** $\sqrt[3]{73} \approx 4.2$

3 a) 0.9   **b)** 0.4   **c)** 1.2   **d)** 0.4

4 40.2

5 a) $3.7^4 \approx 200$ **b)** $2.9^5 \approx 200$ **c)** $1.7^6 \approx 25$

Further

1 $\sqrt{10} > \sqrt{9}$, so $\sqrt{10} > 3$

    $\sqrt[3]{26} < \sqrt[3]{27}$ so $\sqrt[3]{26} < 3$

    $\sqrt{10} > \sqrt[3]{26}$

2 1.9^3 9 3.1^2 10 $\sqrt{103}$

3 a) $\sqrt{16} = 4$ therefore $\sqrt{32} \neq 4$ **b)** $\sqrt{32} \approx 5.7$

4 $\sqrt{3.4^2 + 13 \times 4.8} \approx \sqrt{3^2 + 10 \times 5}$

                  $\approx \sqrt{59}$

                  ≈ 7.7

Pages 10–11
1.2 Fractional indices

Foundations

1 a) 81   **b)** 9   **c)** 3

    d) 1 000 000 000   **e)** 1000   **f)** 10

2 a) 12   **b)** 20   **c)** 3   **d)** 5   **e)** 3

Fluency

1 a) 6   **b)** 10   **c)** 4   **d)** 3   **e)** 1

    f) $\frac{1}{3}$ **g)** $\frac{1}{2}$ **h)** $\frac{1}{2}$ **i)** $\frac{3}{4}$ **j)** $\frac{5}{4}$

2 a) 4   **b)** 64   **c)** 32   **d)** 36

    e) 625   **f)** $\frac{1}{8}$ **g)** $\frac{8}{125}$ **h)** $\frac{16}{9}$

3 a) $\frac{1}{7}$ **b)** $\frac{1}{9}$ **c)** $\frac{216}{125}$ **d)** $\frac{25}{16}$

4 3

Further

1 $4 \times \sqrt{8} = 2^2 \times 2\sqrt{2} = 2^2 \times 2^{\frac{3}{2}} = 2^{\frac{7}{2}}$ so $n = \frac{7}{2}$

2 a) Aaliyah has multiplied 16 by $\frac{3}{2}$

    b) $16^{\frac{3}{2}} = \left((16)^{\frac{1}{2}}\right)^3 = 4^3 = 64$

3 $m^{\frac{4}{3}} = 81$, so $m^{\frac{1}{3}} = 81^{\frac{1}{4}}$, $m^{\frac{1}{3}} = 3$, $m = 27$

4 $\frac{1}{16^{\frac{5}{3}}} = 2^n$, $16^{-\frac{5}{3}} = 2^n$, $(2^4)^{-\frac{5}{3}} = 2^n$, $2^{-\frac{20}{3}} = 2^n$, $n = -\frac{20}{3}$

Pages 12–13
1.3 Upper and lower bounds

Foundations

1 a) 270 **b)** 280 **c)** 280 **d)** 280 **e)** 280 **f)** 290

2 a) 2.4 **b)** 2.5 **c)** 2.5 **d)** 2.5 **e)** 2.5 **f)** 2.6

Fluency

1 a) 13.75 m   **b)** 14.25 m

2 $v = 35.5$ (to 3 significant figures)

3 3 (to 1 significant figure)

Further

1 a) 6.97 metres per second   **b)** 6.73 metres per second

2 Upper bound = 7.0 cm (to 2 significant figures)

    Lower bound = 6.8 cm (to 2 significant figures)

3 34.1 cm (to 3 significant figures)

4 V_{upper} = 5.089 38... m³

           = 5 089 380 cm³

           = 5089.38 litres

    536 buckets

Pages 14–15
1.4 Simplifying surd expressions and rationalising denominators

Foundations

1 a) 1, 2, 3, 4, 6, 8, 12, 16, 24, 48

    b) 1, 2, 4, 5, 8, 10, 16, 20, 40, 80

    c) 1, 2, 4, 8, 16, 32

2 a) 1, 4, 9, 16, 25, 36, 49, 64, 81, 100, 121, 144, 169, 196, 225

b) 1, 8, 27, 64, 125

Fluency

1 **a)** $5\sqrt{3}$ **b)** $10\sqrt{3}$ **c)** $5\sqrt{10}$ **d)** $6\sqrt{2}$ **e)** $4\sqrt{3}$

2 **a)** $\sqrt{200}$ can be further simplified

b) $20\sqrt{2}$

3 $5\sqrt{5}$

4 $24\sqrt{3}$

5 $\dfrac{8\sqrt{3}}{3}$

Further

1 $\dfrac{21 + 3\sqrt{5}}{44}$

2 $\dfrac{4}{\frac{1}{\sqrt{5}} + 1} = \dfrac{4\sqrt{5}}{1 + \sqrt{5}}$

$\dfrac{4\sqrt{5}}{1 + \sqrt{5}} \times \dfrac{1 - \sqrt{5}}{1 - \sqrt{5}} = \dfrac{4\sqrt{5} - 20}{-4}$

$= 5 - \sqrt{5}$

3 $(5 + \sqrt{3})^2 - (5 - \sqrt{3})^2 = 28 + 10\sqrt{3} - (28 - 10\sqrt{3})$

$= 20\sqrt{3}$

4 $w^2 - 6\sqrt{5}w + 45 = z - 72\sqrt{5}$

$6w = 72$, $w = 12$, $144 + 45 = z = 189$

5 $8^2 - (4\sqrt{3})^2 = 16$

$\sqrt{16} = 4$

$\text{Area} = \dfrac{4 \times 4\sqrt{3}}{2}$

$= 8\sqrt{3}$

6 $\sqrt{800}\pi = \sqrt{2}\pi r^2$

$\sqrt{800} = \sqrt{2}r^2$

$\sqrt{400} = r^2$

$20 = r^2$

$r = \sqrt{20} = 2\sqrt{5}$

7 $2\sqrt{3} - 2$, $8 - 4\sqrt{3}$

Pages 16–17
1.5 Converting between recurring decimals and fractions

Foundations

1 **a)** $\dfrac{7}{10}$ **b)** $\dfrac{8}{25}$ **c)** $\dfrac{1}{25}$ **d)** $\dfrac{483}{1000}$ **e)** $\dfrac{101}{125}$

2 **a)** 2.7 **b)** 27 **c)** 270

Fluency

1 $\boxed{\dfrac{1}{3}}$ $\dfrac{2}{5}$ $\boxed{\dfrac{4}{7}}$ $\dfrac{13}{25}$ $\dfrac{3}{8}$ $\boxed{\dfrac{6}{11}}$

2 **a)** $0.\dot{2}$ **b)** $0.\dot{4}$ **c)** $0.\dot{7}$ **d)** $0.\dot{7}1428\dot{5}$

e) $0.\dot{5}\dot{4}$ **f)** $0.1\dot{6}$ **g)** $0.8\dot{3}$

3 **a)** $\dfrac{5}{9}$ **b)** $\dfrac{73}{99}$ **c)** $\dfrac{438}{999}$

d) $\dfrac{6}{90}$ (or equivalent) **e)** $\dfrac{372}{990}$ (or equivalent)

f) $\dfrac{5896}{9990}$ (or equivalent)

4 **a)** $\dfrac{1}{9}$ **b)** $\dfrac{46}{99}$ **c)** $\dfrac{1}{30}$ **d)** $\dfrac{9}{110}$

e) $\dfrac{32}{45}$ **f)** $\dfrac{349}{990}$ **g)** $\dfrac{94}{333}$ **h)** $\dfrac{4153}{9990}$

5 $4\dfrac{1}{15}$

6 $3\dfrac{8}{11}$

7 $1\dfrac{31}{990}$

8 $\sqrt{\dfrac{4}{9}} = \dfrac{2}{3}$

Further

1 $0.\dot{4} \times 0.\dot{8}\dot{1} = \dfrac{4}{9} \times \dfrac{81}{99}$

$= \dfrac{4}{9} \times \dfrac{9}{11}$

$= \dfrac{4}{11}$

2 $0.\dot{3}\dot{6} = \dfrac{4}{11}$

$0.0\dot{3}\dot{6} = \dfrac{4}{110}$

$0.4\dot{3}\dot{6} = \dfrac{4}{10} + \dfrac{4}{110}$

$= \dfrac{24}{55}$

3 $0.\dot{7} - 0.\dot{2}\dot{3} = \dfrac{7}{9} - \dfrac{23}{99}$

$= \dfrac{77}{99} - \dfrac{23}{99}$

$= \dfrac{54}{99}$

$= \dfrac{6}{11}$

4 $\dfrac{12}{99} + \dfrac{1}{3} \div \dfrac{4}{9} = \dfrac{12}{99} + \dfrac{9}{12}$

$= \dfrac{4}{33} + \dfrac{3}{4}$

$= \dfrac{16}{132} + \dfrac{99}{132}$

$= \dfrac{115}{132}$

5 $0.2\dot{8}\dot{5}$ $\dfrac{2}{7} = 0.\dot{2}8571\dot{4}$ $\dfrac{1}{4} = 0.25$ $\dfrac{285}{999} = 0.\dot{2}8\dot{5}$

Therefore, in ascending order:

$\dfrac{1}{4}$ $\dfrac{285}{999}$ $\dfrac{2}{7}$ $0.2\dot{8}\dot{5}$

6 $x = 0.\dot{n}$

$\dfrac{x}{10} = 0.0\dot{n}$

$\dfrac{x}{10} + \dfrac{3}{10} = 0.3\dot{n}$

$0.3\dot{n} = \dfrac{x + 3}{10}$

7 $y = 0.\dot{m}$

$\dfrac{y}{10} = 0.0\dot{m}$

$\dfrac{y}{10} + \dfrac{5}{9} = 0.5\dot{m}$

$\dfrac{9y + 50}{90} = 0.5\dot{m}$

Pages 18–19
1.6 Exact answers

Foundations

1 $A = \pi r^2$

2 $3\sqrt{2}$

Fluency

1 3 hours, 22 minutes and 48 seconds

2 $x = \dfrac{3 + \sqrt{5}}{2}$ or $x = \dfrac{3 - \sqrt{5}}{2}$

3 $8\sqrt{2}$ cm

4 $h = \sqrt{45}$ or $3\sqrt{5}$ cm

5 **a)** 6π **b)** $4\pi + 4$

Further

1 Rectangle: 60 cm²

Isosceles triangle: 12.5 cm²

Answers

Right-hand triangle: $30\,\text{cm}^2$

Proportion shaded: $\frac{60 - 12.5 - 30}{60} = \frac{17.5}{60} = \frac{7}{24}$

2 Two congruent semi-circles form one circle.

Area of circle $= \pi \times \left(\frac{1}{2}\right)^2 = \frac{\pi}{4}$

Area of square $= 1$

Shaded region $= 1 - \frac{\pi}{4}$

Pages 20–21
2F1 Laws of indices
Practice

1 a) $8a^3$ b) $36b^5$ c) $10c^9 + 2c^8$

2 a) d^{16} b) $2f^7$ c) g^{50}

   d) $10h^7$ e) $18y^3z^8$ f) $32n^3x$

   g) $-15t^5$ h) $30f^2$

3 a) j^6 b) $7k^5$ c) $m^{12}n$

   d) $5q^{11}$ e) $\dfrac{5r^6}{8}$ f) 3

   g) $\dfrac{4x}{y}$ h) $\dfrac{5a^{18}}{2b^5}$

4 a) q^{15} b) $r^{0.06}$ c) $h^{\frac{1}{4}}$ d) $27f^9$

5 a) 64 b) 1 c) $\frac{1}{9}$ d) $\frac{81}{100}$

6 a) a^4 b) $\frac{5}{2}m^{10}n$

7 $c = 6$

8 $w = 0$

9 $g^{\frac{37}{60}}$

10 $x = 4$

11 $k = 3$

12 a) 1.37×10^5 b) 1.37×10^7 c) 1.37×10^{-4}

13 a) $45\,700$ b) 0.0457 c) 4050.7

14 a) 4.692×10^4 b) 4.448×10^4

15 a) 6.4×10^5 b) 5×10^{-2}

Pages 22–23
2F2 Equations and changing the subject
Practice

1 a) $x = 12.5$ b) $x = 17.5$ c) $x = 10$ d) $x = 20$

   e) $x = 50$ f) $x = 148$ g) $x = 152$ h) $x = 70$

2 a) $x > 12.5$ b) $x < 17.5$ c) $x \geqslant 10$ d) $x < 20$

   e) $x \geqslant 50$ f) $x < 148$ g) $x \geqslant 152$ h) $x < 70$

3 20

4 12

5 a) $t = 6$ b) $u = -2$ c) $v = -6$

6 a) $a = 1.25$ b) $a = -1.25$

7 a) $y \leqslant 20$ b) $y \geqslant -20$

8 $p = 3$

9 $x = 3$

10 a) $x = zy + w$ b) $x = c(k - a)$

   c) $x = f - dh$ d) $x = \sqrt{\dfrac{m + t}{v}}$

11 $K = \sqrt{\dfrac{V}{t^2}}$

12 $b = \dfrac{2K}{a}$

Pages 24–25
2.1 Changing the subject with unknowns on both sides
Foundations

1 a) $x = \dfrac{y}{r + 3}$

   b) $x = \dfrac{h - 2w}{5}$

   c) $x = \dfrac{5b - 4}{3 - 2m}$

2 a) $x(5 + b)$

   b) $w(h + j)$

   c) $y(a - 1)$

Fluency

1 a) $h = \dfrac{y}{8}$ b) $h = \dfrac{y}{2}$

   c) $h = \dfrac{y}{5 + r}$ d) $h = \dfrac{y}{w - r}$

2 $l = \dfrac{A - 2hw}{2w + 2h}$

3 a) $b = \dfrac{de + 7d}{5c}$

   b) $c = \dfrac{de + 7d}{5b}$

   c) $d = \dfrac{5bc}{e + 7}$

4 a) $y = \dfrac{4x + 9w}{5}$

   b) $y = \dfrac{4x + bw}{b - 4}$

   c) $y = \dfrac{bw - ax}{a + b}$

5 a) $w = \dfrac{p}{D - 1}$ b) $w = \dfrac{Dp}{1 - D}$

6 a) $k = \dfrac{5 - 7m}{m - 1}$ b) $k = \dfrac{5 + 7m}{m - 1}$

   c) $k = \dfrac{7m - 5}{1 + m}$ d) $k = \dfrac{5 - 7m}{1 - m}$

Further

1 $1 + \dfrac{x}{y} = \dfrac{x}{z}$

   $y + x = \dfrac{xy}{z}$

   $yz + xz = xy$

   $xz = y(x - z)$

   $y = \dfrac{xz}{x - z}$

2 a) $pa - b = (a + p)(t - a)$

     $pa - b = at - a^2 + pt - ap$

     $pa + ap - pt = at - a^2 + b$

     $p(2a - t) = at - a^2 + b$

     $p = \dfrac{at - a^2 + b}{2a - t}$

   b) $a(p - t) = t(a - p)$

     $ap - at = ta - tp$

     $ap + tp = 2at$

     $p(a + t) = 2at$

     $p = \dfrac{2at}{a + t}$

   c) $\dfrac{p - a}{p + t} = \dfrac{a^2}{16t^2}$

$$16t^2(p - a) = a^2(p + t)$$
$$16t^2p - 16t^2a = a^2p + a^2t$$
$$16t^2p - a^2p = a^2t + 16t^2a$$
$$p(16t^2 - a^2) = a^2t + 16t^2a$$
$$p = \frac{a^2t + 16t^2a}{16t^2 - a^2}$$

Pages 26–27
2.2 Algebraic fractions
Foundations

1 **a)** $\frac{7}{15}$ **b)** $\frac{7}{10}$ **c)** $\frac{2}{3}$

2 **a)** $6(y + 4)$ **b)** $y(y + 1)$

c) $(x - 6)(x + 4)$ **d)** $(x + 1)(x - 1)$

Fluency

1 **a)** $\frac{7p}{15}$ **b)** $\frac{8p + 10}{15}$

c) $\frac{8p + 1}{15}$ **d)** $\frac{2p + 19}{15}$

2 **a)** $\frac{m}{2}$ **b)** 9 **c)** $\frac{9m^2}{4}$ **d)** $\frac{2m^2}{3}$

3 **a)** $\frac{5x + 11}{(x + 1)(x + 3)}$ **b)** $\frac{5x + 7}{(x - 1)(x + 3)}$

c) $\frac{x - 11}{(x + 1)(x - 3)}$ **d)** $\frac{x - 7}{(x - 1)(x - 3)}$

4 **a)** $\frac{3h^2 + 24h}{20}$ **b)** $\frac{4h + 32}{15h}$

c) $\frac{4h + 32}{15h}$ **d)** $\frac{3h^2 + 24h}{20}$

5 **a)** $\frac{18k - 1}{6}$ **b)** $\frac{-6k - 7}{6}$

c) $\frac{18k - 1}{(3k - 2)(4k + 1)}$ **d)** $\frac{6k + 7}{(3k - 2)(4k + 1)}$

6 **a)** $\frac{(f + 5)(f + 3)}{18}$ **b)** $\frac{f + 5}{f + 3}$

c) 2 **d)** $\frac{18}{(f - 5)(f + 3)}$

7 **a)** $\frac{7}{8}$ **b)** $\frac{1}{12}$ **c)** $\frac{2}{9}$

d) $5x$ **e)** $\frac{x + 5}{x - 1}$ **f)** $\frac{x - 2}{x + 3}$

Further

1 **a)** $\frac{2x + 6}{x^2 + 8x + 15} \times \frac{x^2 + 11x + 28}{x + 4} =$

$\frac{2(x + 3)}{(x + 3)(x + 5)} \times \frac{(x + 4)(x + 7)}{x + 4} = \frac{2x + 14}{x + 5}$

b) $3x + 15 \times \frac{x^2 - 2x + 1}{(x + 5)(x^2 + 4x - 5)} =$

$3(x + 5) \times \frac{(x - 1)^2}{(x + 5)(x + 5)(x - 1)} = \frac{3x - 3}{x + 5}$

c) $\frac{x^2 + 10x + 24}{x^2 - 3x - 28} \div \frac{x^2 + 2x - 24}{x^2 - 16}$

$= \frac{(x + 6)(x + 4)}{(x - 7)(x + 4)} \div \frac{(x + 6)(x - 4)}{(x + 4)(x - 4)}$

$= \frac{(x + 6)(x + 4)}{(x - 7)(x + 4)} \times \frac{(x + 4)(x - 4)}{(x + 6)(x - 4)} = \frac{x + 4}{x - 7}$

2 $\frac{2x^2 + 5x - 12}{x^2 + x - 12} = \frac{(2x - 3)(x + 4)}{(x - 3)(x + 4)} = \frac{2x - 3}{x - 3}$

3 $\frac{y + 3}{15} + \frac{y + 1}{5} + \frac{y}{3} = \frac{y + 3}{15} + \frac{3y + 3}{15} + \frac{5y}{15} = \frac{9y + 6}{15}$

$= \frac{3(3y + 2)}{15}$

Mean: $\frac{3(3y + 2)}{15} \div 3 = \frac{3y + 2}{15}$

4 Difference between terms is $\frac{3}{x + 4} - \frac{2}{x + 3} = \frac{3x + 9 - 2x - 8}{(x + 4)(x + 3)}$

$= \frac{x + 1}{(x + 4)(x + 3)}$

Next term is $\frac{3}{x + 4} + \frac{x + 1}{(x + 4)(x + 3)} = \frac{3(x + 3)}{(x + 4)(x + 3)} +$

$\frac{x + 1}{(x + 4)(x + 3)} = \frac{4x + 10}{(x + 4)(x + 3)} = \frac{2(2x + 5)}{(x + 4)(x + 3)}$

Pages 28–29
2.3 Expanding and factorising
Foundations

1 **a)** $10x - 2$ **b)** $32y - 44$

2 **a)** $2x(3x - 4)$ **b)** $2x(3x - 4 + 2y)$

c) $(x + 2)(x + 3)$ **d)** $(x + 6)(x - 1)$

Fluency

1 **a)** $h^2 + 4h + 3$ **b)** $g^2 + 3g - 10$

c) $k^2 - 5k - 24$ **d)** $m^2 - 12m + 35$

2 **a)** $(3x + 1)(x + 2)$ **b)** $(2x + 3)(x + 5)$

c) $(5x + 4)(x + 3)$ **d)** $(2x + 7)(2x + 1)$

3 **a)** $3t^2 + 2t - 5$ **b)** $6u^2 - 13u + 6$

c) $2p^2 - 18$ **d)** $24 - 2h^2 - 2h$

4 **a)** $4x^2 - 9$ **b)** $25 - k^2$

c) $36u^2 - 121$ **d)** $x^2 + 8x + 16$

e) $y^2 - 12y + 36$ **f)** $49h^2 - 126h + 81$

5 **a)** $(2x + 9)(x - 2)$

b) $(3b + 8)(b - 3)$

c) $(2y - 2)(3y + 4)$ or $2(y - 1)(3y + 4)$ or $(y - 1)(6y + 8)$

d) $(2x + 6)(x - 3)$ or $(2x - 6)(x + 3)$ or $2(x + 3)(x - 3)$

e) $(3x - 9)(3x + 9)$ **or** $9(x + 3)(x - 3)$

f) $(12y - 13a)(12y + 13a)$

g) $\left(\frac{2}{5}n - \frac{9}{10}\right)\left(\frac{2}{5}n + \frac{9}{10}\right)$

h) $\left(8a - \frac{1}{2}b\right)\left(8a + \frac{1}{2}b\right)$

6 **a)** $y^2 + by + ay + ab$ **b)** $y^2 - b^2$

c) $y^2 - by - ay + ab$ **d)** $ay + ab - y^2 - by$

e) $y^2 + 2ay + a^2$ **f)** $y^2 - 2by + b^2$

Further

1 **a)** $(3t - 2)(t + 1) = (3t^2 + t - 2)\,\text{m}^2$

b) $(u - 5)^2 = (u^2 - 10u + 25)\,\text{cm}^2$

2 **a)** $(-2x - 5)(x - 4)$ **b)** $(3xy + 1)(x - 2)$

c) $(-2x + 3)(2x - 8)$ **d)** $(-3x - 2)(xy - y)$

3 $(x + g)(3x + h) = 3x^2 - 48$

$3x^2 + hx + 3gx + gh = 3x^2 - 48$

$gh = -48$ and $hx + 3gx = 0$

$g = 4, h = -12$

$g = -4, h = 12$

4 $9x^2 - 48x + 64 = (3x - 8)^2$

Side length $= 3x - 8$

Perimeter $= 4(3x - 8) = 12x - 32$

Pages 30–31
2.4 Algebraic proof

Foundations

1 a) $12n$ **b)** $4n^2 - 4n + 1$

2 a) $2(2n^2 + 2n + 1)$ **b)** $(n + 2)(n + 2)$ or $(n + 2)^2$

Fluency

1 a) Even **b)** Odd **c)** Cannot tell **d)** Even
  e) Cannot tell **f)** Cannot tell **g)** Cannot tell **h)** Even

2 a) $(2n)^2 \equiv 4n^2$, which is a multiple of 4, therefore divisible by 4

  b) $2n + 1$

  c) $(2n + 1)^2 \equiv (2n + 1)(2n + 1)$
    $\equiv 4n^2 + 4n + 1$
    $\equiv 4(n^2 + n) + 1$

    $4(n^2 + n)$ is a multiple of 4, so is even. $4(n^2 + n) + 1$ must therefore be an odd number and cannot be even.

3 $(2n + 1)(2m + 1) \equiv 4mn + 2m + 2n + 1 \equiv 2(2mn + m + n) + 1$, which is 1 more than a multiple of 2

4 $(3n + 1)^2 - (3n - 1)^2 \equiv 9n^2 + 6n + 1 - (9n^2 - 6n + 1)$
    $\equiv 9n^2 + 6n + 1 - 9n^2 + 6n - 1$
    $\equiv 12n$, which is always a multiple of 12

5 $(2n)^2 + (2n + 2)^2 \equiv 4n^2 + 4n^2 + 8n + 4$
    $\equiv 8n^2 + 8n + 4$
    $\equiv 4(2n^2 + 2n + 1)$, which is always a multiple of 4

6 $(n + 4)(n + 3) + (n + 4) \equiv (n + 4)(n + 3 + 1) \equiv (n + 4)(n + 4) \equiv (n + 4)^2$, so is always a square number

Further

1 The sum of two consecutive integers: $n + n + 1 \equiv 2n + 1$

The difference between the squares of the integers:
$(n + 1)^2 - n^2 \equiv n^2 + 2n + 1 - n^2 \equiv 2n + 1$, which is the same as the sum of two consecutive integers so this statement is true for all values of n.

2 $(2n)^2 + (2m)^2 \equiv 4n^2 + 4m^2 \equiv 4(n^2 + m^2)$, which is always a multiple of 4

3 $(2n + 1)^2 - (2m + 1)^2 \equiv 4n^2 + 4n + 1 - (4m^2 + 4m + 1)$
$\equiv 4n^2 + 4n - 4m^2 - 4m \equiv 4(n^2 + n - m^2 - m)$, which is always a multiple of 4

4 $(2n + 1)^2 + (2n + 3)^2 \equiv 4n^2 + 4n + 1 + 4n^2 + 12n + 9 \equiv 8n^2 + 16n + 10 \equiv 8(n^2 + 2n + 1) + 2$

$8(n^2 + 2n + 1)$ is a multiple of 8, therefore $8(n^2 + 2n + 1) + 2$ is always 2 greater than a multiple of 8

5 $(2n + 1)^2 + (2n + 3)^2 + (2n + 5)^2 \equiv 12n^2 + 36n + 35$
    $\equiv 12(n^2 + 3n + 3) - 1$

Pages 32–33
2.5 Functions

Foundations

1 a) 16 **b)** −15 **c)** 9 **d)** 36 **e)** 4

2 a) $x = 4$ **b)** $x = 4.2$
  c) $x = 25$ **d)** $x = 35$

Fluency

1 a) $f^{-1}(x) = \dfrac{x - 2}{2}$
  b) $g^{-1}(x) = 4x + 3$
  c) $h^{-1}(x) = \sqrt{x + 3}$

2 a) 16 **b)** 58 **c)** $x = 4$ or -4

3 a) 0.4 **b)** 6.4

4 a) 82 **b)** 162

5 a) 5 **b)** 4 **c)** 0

Further

1 a) $fg(3) = f(9) = 19$
  b) $gf(x) = g(2x + 1) = (2x + 1)^2 = 4x^2 + 4x + 1$

2 $x^2 = 5x - 6$, so $x^2 - 5x + 6 = 0$
  $(x - 3)(x - 2) = 0$
  $x = 3, x = 2$

3 $fg(x) = f(2x) = 5(2x) + 6 = 10x + 6$
  $10x + 6 = 50$, gives $x = 4.4$

4 $h(x + 2) = (x + 2)^2 + 1 = x^2 + 4x + 5$

5 $f(x + 1) = (x + 1)^2 + 3 = x^2 + 2x + 4$
  $f(x + 1) + f(x) = x^2 + 2x + 4 + x^2 + 3 = 2x^2 + 2x + 7$

Pages 34–35
2.6 Parallel and perpendicular lines

Foundations

  a) 2, (0, 4) **b)** −3, (0, 5) **c)** 3, (0, 5)
  d) $-\frac{1}{2}$, (0, 2.5) **e)** $-\frac{3}{2}$, (0, −3)

Fluency

1 $y = 3x +$ any constant

2 $y = 6x + 4$

3 $y = -\frac{3}{2}x - 1$ (or equivalent)

4 a) $-\frac{1}{2}$ **b)** $\frac{1}{5}$ **c)** $\frac{1}{3}$ **d)** −8

5 $y = \frac{1}{3}x - 5$

6 $y = \frac{1}{2}x + 12.5$

7 $y = -\frac{5}{2}x + 15$

Further

1 a) D **b)** B and C
  c) A and B **d)** A and C, B and C

2 Gradient of $3y = x + 12$ is $\frac{1}{3}$
  Gradient of $5y + 2x = 20$ is $-\frac{2}{5}$
  $\frac{1}{3} \times -\frac{2}{5} \neq -1$, hence not perpendicular

3 a) Gradient = −1; Equation: $y = -x + 7$
  b) Perpendicular gradient is 1
    Midpoint is (1, 6)
    Equation is $y = x + 5$

4 Gradient of p is $-\frac{1}{2}$ and gradient of q is 6
  $-\frac{1}{2} \times 6 \neq -1$ so not perpendicular

5 PQ has gradient −2. So, PR needs gradient $\frac{1}{2}$
  $\dfrac{a - 10}{9 - 5} = \dfrac{1}{2}$
  So $a - 10 = 2$, so $a = 12$

Pages 36–37
2.7 Quadratic graphs
Foundations

  a) $x = -3$, $x = -2$ **b)** $x = 4$, $x = 3$ **c)** $x = -5$, $x = 2$

Fluency

1 **a)** $(0, 8)$

  b) $x = -2$, $x = -4$

  c) $y = (x + 3)^2 - 1$, so at $(-3, -1)$

  d) $x = -3$

  e)

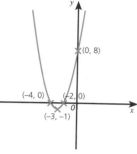

2 **a)** $(0, -15)$, $x = 3$ and $x = -5$, $(x + 1)^2 - 16$, giving $(-1, -16)$

    $x = -1$ is line of symmetry

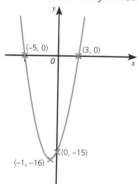

  b) $(0, -49)$, $x = 7$ and $x = -7$, already in completed square form

    Vertex at $(0, -49)$

    $x = 0$ is the line of symmetry

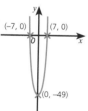

3 **a)** $(0, 4)$

  b) $x = 1$, $x = -4$

  c) $y = -(x + 1.5)^2 + 6.25$

    Vertex at $(-1.5, 6.25)$

  d)

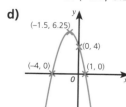

Further

1 **a)** $(0, 64)$

  b) $(x + 8)(x + 8) = 0$, giving $x = -8$, twice

    So the graph touches the x-axis at $(-8, 0)$, meaning that is where the minimum point must be.

  c)

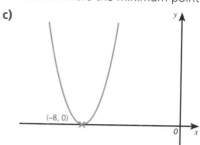

2

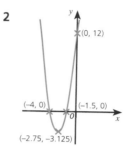

3 **a)** You need to square root a negative number, so it doesn't work.

  b) This means the graph doesn't cross the x-axis.

  c) $(x + 2)^2 + 6$ giving vertex at $(-2, 6)$

  d)

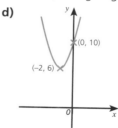

Pages 38–39
2.8 Other functions
Foundations

  a) 9   **b)** $\frac{1}{9}$ **c)** $\frac{1}{8}$

Fluency

1 **a)** Values are $\frac{1}{3}$, 1, 3, 9, 27

  b)

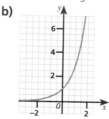

  c) Approx. 2.5

    Answers are approximate since they involve reading from a graph.

2 **a)** 53° and 307°

  b) 114° and 246°

3 a) 54° and 234°

b) 153° and 333°

4 1.2 and 5 since sine values must be between −1 and 1

Further

1 $(0, 6) \rightarrow 6 = a \times b^0$, so $a = 6$

$(1, 24) \rightarrow 24 = 6 \times b^1$, so $b = 4$

The equation is $y = 6 \times 4^x$

When $x = 2$, $y = 96$, so $c = 96$

2 a)

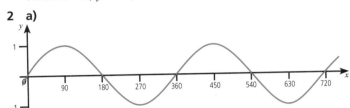

b) Approx. values: 17°, 163°, 377° and 523°

Pages 40–41
2.9 Transformations of graphs

Foundations

a)

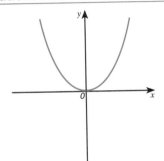

b)

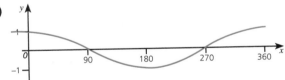

c)

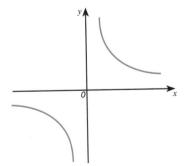

Fluency

1 a) C   **b)** A   **c)** D   **d)** B

2 a) and **b)**

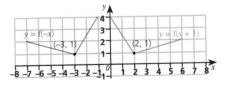

3 a) (−1, −10)   **b)** (−4, −6)   **c)** (1, −6)

4 $y = f(x − 3)$

Further

1 a) (−1, 0), (−4, 0) and (3, 0)

b) (−2, 0), (2, 0) and (5, 0)

2

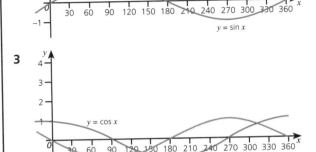

3

4 Translated 2 units to the left **and** 3 units down

(0, −2)

Pages 42–43
2.10 Estimating area

Foundations

88 cm²

Fluency

1 a) A: 1.5 m/s²   B: 0   C: 1 m/s²   D: −1.25 m/s²

b) 675 m

2 a) Approx. 27.8 m

b) An underestimate because the areas are all below the actual curve

3 a) 4 seconds   **b)** Approx. 26.5 m

Further

1 a) 38.5   **b)** Use more strips

2 a) Approx. 2.75   **b)** 1.5

Pages 44–45
2.11 Equations of circles

Foundations

1 −5

2 −4

Fluency

1 a) 6

b) 16 + 4 does not equal 36, so it doesn't lie on the circle

c) $y = 2\sqrt{5}$ or $y = −2\sqrt{5}$

2 a) $x^2 + y^2 = 25$

b) Yes, 16 + 9 does equal 25

3 $x^2 + y^2 = 4$

4

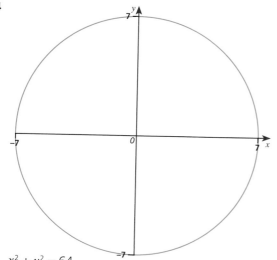

5 $x^2 + y^2 = 64$

Further

1 a) $(0, 0)$ **b)** $x^2 + y^2 = 25$

2 $x^2 + y^2 = 169$

3 a) $2\sqrt{5}$

   b) Gradient of radius = 2, gradient of tangent = $-\frac{1}{2}$

      Equation of tangent is $y = -\frac{1}{2}x + 5$

4 a) Gradient of radius = $-\frac{3}{2}$, gradient of tangent = $\frac{2}{3}$

      Equation of tangent is $y = \frac{2}{3}x + \frac{13}{3}$

   b) Set $y = 0$ and solve. Gives $x = -6.5$

Pages 46–47
2.12 Quadratic equations
Foundations

   a) $x = 5, x = 2$ **b)** $x = 6, x = -3$ **c)** $x = -8, x = -4$

Fluency

1 a) 0.16, –3.16   **b)** 1.20, –1.45   **c)** 4.32, –2.32

2 a) $-1 \pm 2\sqrt{2}$ **b)** $-3 \pm 2\sqrt{5}$ **c)** $2 \pm \sqrt{5}$

3 1.58, –0.380

4 0.4, –8.4

5 a) $x(x + 12) = 48$

      $x^2 + 12x = 48$

      $x^2 + 12x - 48 = 0$

   b) $x = 3.17$ or -15.1

      Discount negative, since length can't be negative.

      $x = 3.17$ and $x + 12 = 15.17$

Further

1 a) $5(2x + 4) + (2x - 2)(x + 1) = 33$

      $10x + 20 + 2x^2 - 2x + 2x - 2 = 33$

      $2x^2 + 10x - 15 = 0$

   b) $x = 1.21, x = -6.21$

      Discount negative values, so $x = 1.21$

2 a) $(x + 3)^2 + (2x - 1)^2 = (2x + 4)^2$

      $x^2 + 6x + 9 + 4x^2 - 4x + 1 = 4x^2 + 16x + 16$

      $x^2 - 14x - 6 = 0$

   b) Solve to give $x = 14.4$ and $x = -0.416$

      Discount negative solution, so $x = 14.4$

   c) Perimeter is $5x + 6$; when $x = 14.4$, perimeter is 78 cm

3 $\frac{1}{2}(a + b)h = \frac{1}{2}(3x - 1 + x + 3) \times (x + 2) = 75$

    $\frac{1}{2}(4x + 2)(x + 2) = 75$

    $(4x + 2)(x + 2) = 150$

    $4x^2 + 8x + 2x + 4 = 150$

    $4x^2 + 10x - 146 = 0$

    $2x^2 + 5x - 73 = 0$

    Solving gives $x = 4.92$ and $x = -7.42$

    Discount the negative solution, so $x = 4.92$

Pages 48–49
2.13 Completing the square
Foundations

1 a) $x^2 + 8x + 16$ **b)** $x^2 + 24x + 144$ **c)** $x^2 - 10x + 25$

2 a) $x = -3, x = 2$ **b)** $x = 5$ (twice)   **c)** $x = 6, x = 4$

Fluency

1 a) No   **b)** No   **c)** Yes, $(x + 4)^2$ **d)** Yes, $(x - 4)^2$

2 a) $(x + 6)^2$ **b)** $(x - 5)^2$ **c)** $(x - 2)^2$

3 a) $(x + 4)^2 - 6$ **b)** $(x + 4)^2 + 4$

   c) $(x + 4)^2 - 26$ **d)** $(x + 2)^2 + 3$

   e) $(x - 2)^2 + 16$ **f)** $(x - 3)^2 - 11$

4 a) $p = 5, q = -19$ **b)** $x = -5 + \sqrt{19}, x = -5 - \sqrt{19}$

5 $x = 3 + 2\sqrt{2}, x = 3 - 2\sqrt{2}$

Further

1 $2x^2 + 16x + 5 \equiv 2(x^2 + 8x) + 5 \equiv 2[(x + 4)^2 - 16] + 5 \equiv 2(x + 4)^2 - 27$

2 $(x + 7)^2 - 19$

   The minimum value of $x^2 + 14x + 30$ occurs when $x = -7$

   The minimum value of $x^2 + 14x + 30$ is -19

3 $x^2 + 2x + 5 \equiv (x + 1)^2 + 4$

   Turning point when $x = -1$, which gives $y = 4$, so $(-1, 4)$

Pages 50–51
2.14 Simultaneous equations with a quadratic
Foundations

1 $x = 2, y = 4$

2 a) $x = 4, x = 5$ **b)** $x = 4, x = -2$

Fluency

   a) $x = 4, y = 2$ and $x = -4, y = -2$

   b) $x = 1, y = 2$ and $x = -1, y = 0$

   c) $x = 4, y = 6$ and $x = -6, y = -4$

   d) $x = 1, y = 3$ and $x = -\frac{2}{3}, y = \frac{4}{3}$

   e) $x = 6, y = 3$ and $x = \frac{3}{17}, y = -\frac{114}{17}$

Further

1 a) $x = 5, y = -\frac{1}{2}$ and $x = -1, y = 1$

   b) $x = 4, y = 1$ and $x = 1, y = 4$

   c) $x = 2, y = 7$ and $x = -1, y = 1$

2 a) A(3, 4)   B(4, 3)

   b) Length = $\sqrt{2}$

Pages 52–53
2.15 Iteration
Foundations

a) 1.91 **b)** 2.80 **c)** −1.26

Fluency

1 $x = 2$ gives −6 and $x = 3$ gives 8. There is a change of sign. 0 lies between −6 and 8 and so there is a solution between $x = 2$ and $x = 3$

2 $x_2 = 3.3333$, $x_3 = 4.8$, $x_4 = 5.1666$

3 a) $6x^2 - 7x - 2 = 0$

$$6x^2 = 7x + 2$$
$$x^2 = \frac{7x + 2}{6}$$
$$x = \sqrt{\frac{7x + 2}{6}}$$

b) Gives: 1.22, 1.33, 1.37, 1.39, 1.40, 1.40, so 1.40 to 2 d.p.

4 a) $x = 0$ gives −1, $x = 1$ gives 2. There is a change of sign, so a solution lies between 0 and 1

b) $x^3 + 2x - 1 = 0$

$$2x = 1 - x^3$$
$$x = \frac{1}{2}(1 - x^3)$$

c) 0.4375, 0.458, 0.452

Further

1 B and D

2 a) $x^3 + 7x - 5 = 0$

$$x^3 + 7x = 5$$
$$x(x^2 + 7) = 5$$
$$x = \frac{5}{x^2 + 7}$$

b) 0.625, 0.677, 0.670

c) Substituting in gives −0.005 49, which is very close to 0, so the answer is accurate.

3 $x_1 = 1$ gives 1.73 for the first iteration, but then $10 - 7 \times 1.73$ is negative and can't be square rooted.

Pages 54–55
2.16 Two or more inequalities
Foundations

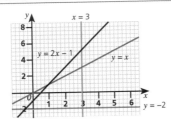

Fluency

1 a)

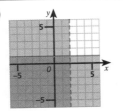

b)

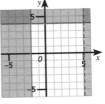

c)

d)

e)

2 a)

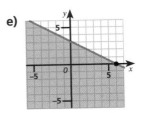

b)

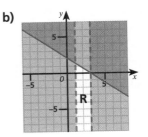

Further

1 a) $y > x$ **b)** $y \leqslant 2$ **c)** $3x + 2y > 6$ **d)** $y < 2x + 1$

2 a)

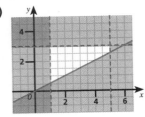

b) (2, 1), (2, 2), (3, 2), (4, 2)

3 $y < 2x + 2$, $x \leqslant 3$, $y > -3$

Pages 56–57
2.17 Quadratic inequalities
Foundations

   a) $x = -1, x = -2$ **b)** $x = -5, x = 2$ **c)** $x = 3, x = 5$

Fluency

1 **a)** $x < -5, x > 6$

     In set notation $\{x: x < -5\} \cup \{x: x > 6\}$

  b) $-5 \leqslant x \leqslant 7$

     In set notation $\{x: -5 \leqslant x \leqslant 7\}$

  c) $x \leqslant -10, x \geqslant 10$

     In set notation $\{x: x \leqslant -10\} \cup \{x: x \geqslant 10\}$

  d) $-4 < x < 5$

     In set notation $\{x: -4 < x < 5\}$

  e) $x < -2.5, x > -1$

     In set notation $\{x: x < -2.5\} \cup \{x: x > -1\}$

2 $x^2 + x - 12 > 0$

Further

1 $x < 2 - \sqrt{3}, x > 2 + \sqrt{3}$

    In set notation $\{x: x < 2 - \sqrt{3}\} \cup \{x: x > 2 + \sqrt{3}\}$

2 First inequality gives: $x < -10, x > 10$

    Second inequality gives: $-12 \leqslant x \leqslant 4$

    Both true for $-12 \leqslant x < -10$

3 Critical values are -1.32 and 8.32

    Inequality is $-1.32 < x < 8.32$

    Integer values in this range are: $-1, 0, 1, 2, 3, 4, 5, 6, 7, 8$

Pages 58–59
2.18 Geometric sequences

Foundations

   a) 19   **b)** 48   **c)** 0.875

Fluency

1 C

2 **a)** 405, 1215

  b) 64, −128

  c) $\frac{2}{27}, \frac{2}{81}$

  d) $\frac{1}{9}, -\frac{1}{27}$

  e) $36, 36\sqrt{3}$

3 3, 12, 48, 192

4 $2, 1, \frac{1}{2}, \frac{1}{4}$

Further

1 **a)** 4   **b)** 768, 3072

  c) $3 \times 4^{n-1}$ **d)** 256

2 $192, 384\sqrt{2}$

3 **a)** $6 \times (-2)^{n-1}$ **b)** $3 \times (\sqrt{7})^{n-1}$

4 **a)** 8, 6.4, 5.12, 4.096

  b) Because each time you multiply the previous height by 0.8, so it is a geometric sequence with common ratio 0.8

  c) 2.62144 m

  d) No, because the ball won't ever stop bouncing in this model

Pages 60–61
2.19 Quadratic sequences
Foundations

1 **a)** −1, −7, −13, −19   **b)** 3, 6, 11, 18

2 **a)** $4n - 1$ **b)** $10 - 2n$

Fluency

1 **a)** 57, 74   **b)** 45, 66

2 **a)** 3, 8, 15, 24

  b) −1, 5, 15, 29   **c)** 0, 1, 4, 9

3 **a)** $2n^2$ **b)** $n^2 + 1$ **c)** $n^2 - 3$

4 $n^2 + 3n - 1$

Further

1 $61 - 23 = 38$

2 **a)** $n^2 + 3n + 1$

  b) $2n^2 + 2n - 1$

  c) $n^2 + n + 13$

3 **a)** $n^2 + n + 3$

  b) $n^2 + n + 3 = 59$

    $n^2 + n - 56 = 0$

    $(n + 8)(n - 7) = 0$

    $n = -8, n = 7$

    n represents the position so can't be negative, $n = 7$

Pages 62–63
3F1 Relationships with ratio
Practice

1

Number of cups	1	3	4	11
Cost	£1.90	£5.70	£7.60	£20.90

2 **a)** £90   **b)** £25   **c)** £166.67

3 Graphs **A** and **D** should be ticked.

4 B

5

p	3	5	10	40	60	100
q	7.8	13	26	104	156	260

6 **a)** 4.5 hours   **b)** 27 hours   **c)** 6.75 hours

    Everybody works at the same rate

7 All the values are the same (40)

8 **a)** 2100   **b)** 200 minutes = 3 hours 20 minutes

9 10.8

10 **a)** 281   **b)** 140

Pages 64–65
3.1 Complex ratio problems
Foundations

1 6 : 15 : 10

2 £15

Fluency

1 70

2 $\frac{20}{39}$

3 22.5%

4 $20 : 15 : 63 : 42$

5 18

Further

1 Before cubes are added:

number of blue cubes : number of red cubes $= 1:4$

After blue cubes are added:

number of blue cubes : number of red cubes $= 3:5$

The number of red cubes remains constant so taking equivalent fractions using the LCM of 4 and 5:

$1:4 = 5:20$

$3:5 = 12:20$

$5 + 20 = 25$

$12 + 20 = 32$

$25:32$

2 $\frac{a-b}{a+b} = \frac{k}{1}$

$a - b = ak + bk$

$a - ak = bk + b$

$a(1 - k) = bk + b$

$a = \frac{bk + b}{1 - k}$

3 $\frac{x^2}{3x - 4} = \frac{2}{1}$

$x^2 = 6x - 8$

$x^2 - 6x + 8 = 0$

$(x - 2)(x - 4) = 0$

$x = 2$ or $x = 4$

4 $3.5 \div 5 \times 8 = 5.6$

$\frac{3.5 + 4 \times 5.6}{5} = 5.18$ g per cm³

Pages 66–67

3.2 Direct and inverse proportion equations

Foundations

a) 2000 **b)** 2 **c)** $2\sqrt{2}$

Fluency

1 a) $g = 4h$ **b)** $g = 32$ **c)** $h = \frac{6}{4} = \frac{3}{2}$

2 a) $p = 20$ **b)** $s = \frac{6}{5}$

3 a) $y = 260$ **b) i)** $x = 20$ **ii)** $x = \frac{4}{5}$

4 a) $p = \frac{14}{3}r$ **b)** $p = 224$ **c)** $r = \frac{15}{14}$

5 a) $t = 3\sqrt{s}$ **b)** $t = \frac{96}{\sqrt[3]{s}}$ **c)** $t = \frac{3}{32768}s^3$

6 a) $x = 2$ **b)** $x = \sqrt{7}$

Further

1 $x = \frac{5}{2}\sqrt[3]{y}$ $z = \frac{75}{x^2}$

When $y = 3.375$, $x = \frac{5}{2}\sqrt[3]{3.375} = \frac{15}{4}$

$z = \frac{75}{\left(\frac{15}{4}\right)^2} = \frac{16}{3}$

2 a) Area $= \pi \times$ radius² so the area is directly proportional to the square of the radius, with constant of proportionality π

b) $V = kr^3$

$524 = 125k$

$V = 4.192r^3$

$V = 4.192 \times 11^3 = 5579.6$ cm³ (to 1 d.p.)

3 a) $m = \frac{k}{\sqrt{p}}$

$2 = \frac{k}{\sqrt{48}}$

$2 = \frac{k}{\sqrt{16} \times \sqrt{3}}$

$2 = \frac{k}{4\sqrt{3}}$

$k = 8\sqrt{3}$

$m = \frac{8\sqrt{3}}{\sqrt{p}} = \frac{8\sqrt{3p}}{p}$

b) $8\sqrt{5} = \frac{8\sqrt{3p}}{p}$

$\sqrt{5} = \frac{\sqrt{3p}}{p}$

$p\sqrt{5} = \sqrt{3p}$

$5p^2 = 3p$

$5p^2 - 3p = 0$

$p(5p - 3) = 0$

$p = \frac{3}{5}$ (p cannot be equal to 0 as m and p are inversely proportional)

Pages 68–69

3.3 Gradient at a point

Foundations

$\frac{5 - -3}{6 - 2} = \frac{8}{4} = 2$

Fluency

1 a) i) Approx. -0.8 m/s

   ii) At 4 seconds, the ball is falling at 0.8 metres per second (or equivalent statement)

b) $m = \frac{y_2 - y_1}{x_2 - x_1}$

$= \frac{6.6 - 3.4}{3 - 1}$

$= 1.6$ m/s

2 a) $m = \frac{y_2 - y_1}{x_2 - x_1}$

$= \frac{18 - 0}{2.5 - 0}$

$= 7.2$ mph

b) i) Choose a point on the curve between $t = 1.7$ and $t = 2.3$ and draw a tangent.

Rate of change in the range 14.5 mph to 15 mph

   ii) The answer to part i) is only an estimate as it was calculated using a hand-drawn tangent, which may not be accurate.

3 a) 3 **b)** It is instantaneously at rest/stationary

Further

a) Estimate for temperature at 2 minutes between 74°C and 76°C

Estimate for temperature at 10 minutes between 38°C and 40°C

Estimate for the rate of change between 4.25°C per minute and 4.75°C per minute.

b) Draws a tangent at time = 2 minutes

Attempts to calculate gradient of tangent by drawing a right-angled triangle and using $m = \dfrac{y_2 - y_1}{x_2 - x_1}$

Estimates the gradient as between −8.7 and −9.2 and/or interprets the instantaneous rate of change as a decrease of between 8.7°C per minute and 9.2°C per minute.

c) Samira is incorrect because eventually the temperature will reach that of the room, at which point the gradient will be 0.

Pages 70–71
4F1 All about angles
Practice

1 **a)** $a = 33°$ **b)** $b = 150°$ **c)** $c = 147°$
2 **a)** $x = 45°$ **b)** $x = 66.5°$ **c)** $x = 279°$
3 **a)** $w = 161°$ **b)** $x = 79°$ **c)** $y = 98°$ **d)** $z = 98°$
4 $v = 78°$ Corresponding angles are equal
   $w = 83°$ Angles on a straight line sum to 180° and corresponding angles are equal
   $x = 19°$ Angles in a triangle sum to 180°
   (Other reasoning is possible)
5 **a)** AB and CD are parallel **b)** No parallel lines
6 $3x − 15 + 2x + 40 = 180$ $x = 31$
7 **a)** $y = 130.5°$ **b)** $x = 61°$
8 **a)** $n = 12$ **b)** $n = 24$ **c)** $n = 16$
9 **a)** $n = 5$ **b)** $n = 10$ **c)** $n = 20$
10 **a)** $x = 129°$ **b)** $x = 286°$ **c)** $x = 120°$
11 $y = 36°$

Pages 72–73
4F2 Describing transformations
Practice

1 **a)** Reflection in the line $x = 1$
   b) Rotation, 180°, about the origin
   c) Translation by $\begin{pmatrix} 2 \\ 4 \end{pmatrix}$
   d) Enlargement, scale factor 2, centre (2, −3)
2 **a)** Reflection in the line $y = x$
   b) Reflection in the line $y = −x$
   c) Enlargement, scale factor $\frac{1}{2}$, centre (−2, 4)
   d) Rotation, 90° anticlockwise, about (0, 0)
   e) Enlargement, scale factor $\frac{3}{2}$, centre (2, 6)
3 Example answer: She has not described a single transformation. Rotation of 180° about (3.5, 3)
4 **a)** Translation by $\begin{pmatrix} 4 \\ -4 \end{pmatrix}$
   b) Reflection in the line $y = x$
   c) Rotation, 90° anticlockwise, about (2, 2)
      or
      Rotation, 90° clockwise, about (−2, −2)
      (**or** 270° in the other direction)
   d) Reflection in the line $y = x$

Pages 74–75
4F3 Basic trigonometry
Practice

1 **a)** $x = 16.472$ **b)** $x = 16.472$ **c)** $x = 411.8$
2 **a)** $a = 9.58\,m$ **b)** $b = 11.7\,cm$ **c)** $c = 5.69\,m$
   d) $d = 9.21\,cm$ **e)** $e = 13.1\,mm$ **f)** $f = 27.1\,m$
3 **a)** $\theta = 49.3°$ **b)** $\theta = 35.5°$ **c)** $\theta = 31.6°$
   d) $\theta = 56.7°$ **e)** $\theta = 63.4°$ **f)** $\theta = 12.9°$
4 **a)** $p = 5.22\,m$ **b)** $p = 5.80\,m$ **c)** $p = 57.4°$
   d) $p = 61.7°$ **e)** $p = 8.86\,m$
5 **a)** $x = 29.2\,cm$ **b)** $x = 3.06\,m$
6 CB = 11.57 cm   BD = 2.25 cm
7 **a)** $x = 5$ $y = 5\sqrt{3}$ **b)** $x = 4\sqrt{2}$ $y = 4\sqrt{2}$

Pages 76–77
4.1 Negative enlargement
Foundations

   a) 18 cm **b)** 1.5 cm

Fluency

1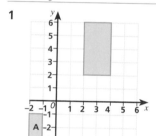

2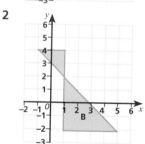

3 Enlargement, scale factor −4, centre (−3, −2)
4 Enlargement, scale factor $-\frac{1}{3}$, centre (3, 3.5)

Further

1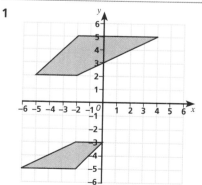

2 Enlargement, scale factor −1, centre (−7, 4)

Pages 78–79
4.2 Invariance

Foundations

l_1 is $y = 4$, l_2 is $x = -\frac{3}{2}$, l_3 is $y = 3x + 2$, l_4 is $y = -x - 1$

Fluency

1 a) A **b)** C **c)** B and D **d)** A and C

2 a) P and S **b)** $x + y = 8$

Further

1 a) Example answer: Enlargement, scale factor 2, centre (1, 1)

b) Example answer: Reflection in the line $y = 3x - 2$

c) Example answer: Reflection in the line $y = -2x + 8$

2 Example answer: Each of the vertices of rectangle A have been translated by column vector $\begin{pmatrix} 3 \\ -2 \end{pmatrix}$

3 A translation by $\begin{pmatrix} 0 \\ 0 \end{pmatrix}$

4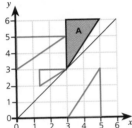

(3, 3) is the point of invariance.

Pages 80–81
4.3 Circle theorems (1)

Foundations

a) $x = 42°$ **b)** $k = 38°$ **c)** $m = 66°$ **d)** $n = 58°$

Fluency

1 a) $a = 75°$ **b)** $b = 106°$

2 a) $c = 36°$ **b)** $d = 45°$ **c)** $e = 30°$

3 a) $f = 29°$ **b)** $g = 52°$ and $h = 52°$

4 a) $i = 56°$ **b)** $j = 93°$ and $k = 84°$ **c)** $l = 39°$

Further

1 Angle ZOY = 74° (angle at the centre is twice the angle at the circumference)

$\frac{180 - 74}{2} = 53°$

2 $90° - 57° (= 33°)$

$x = 33°$ (angles in the same segment are equal)

3 BOC = 118° (angle at the centre is twice the angle at the circumference)

4 $4m + 104 = 180$

$m = 19°$

$q = 38°$

Pages 82–83
4.4 Circle theorems (2)

Foundations

a) $a = 25°$ **b)** $b = 82.5°$ **c)** $c = 50°$ **d)** $d = 83°$

Fluency

1 37°

2 48°

3 29°

4 $x = 53.5°$ $y = 53.5°$

Further

1 a) 14°

The angle between a tangent and a radius is 90°

b) 76°

The angle between a tangent and a chord is equal to the angle in the alternate segment.

2 $180 - \frac{x}{2}$

3 ∠ABD = ∠ACD Angles in the same segment are equal

∠BAD = ∠CDA The angle in a semi-circle is 90°

BOD = AOC

Triangles are congruent, ASA

Pages 84–85
4.5 Congruence

Foundations

a) AB **b)** CB **c)** 10 cm

Fluency

(Other reasoning is possible)

1 $4^2 + 3^2 = 25$

$5^2 = 25$

The triangles are congruent as all corresponding sides are of equal length and corresponding angles are all equal.

2 ∠ABC = ∠ADC

Sides AB = BC = AD = CD

Therefore, the triangles satisfy the congruency condition SAS.

3 Straight line drawn connecting K and M

MJ = KL and JK = ML and the triangles share a common side KM.

Therefore, the triangles are congruent as they satisfy the congruency condition SSS.

4 Sides PT = TQ = ST = TR and angles STR and PTQ are equal, vertically opposite angles.

The triangles satisfy the congruency condition SAS.

Further

(Other reasoning is possible)

1 Angles GEO and GFO are both 90° (a tangent meets a radius at 90°).

The triangles share the side GO, which is opposite the right angles (the hypotenuse).

EO and FO is the radius of the circle with centre O.

Therefore, the triangles satisfy the congruency condition RHS (right angle, hypotenuse, side).

2 CD = FD as D is the midpoint of CF.

Angles EFD and BDC are equal as they are corresponding angles.

AE = EF, therefore BD = EF as AE and BD are equal, opposite sides of a parallelogram.

Therefore, the triangles satisfy the congruency condition SAS.

Pages 86–87
4.6 Similar areas and volumes
Foundations

1 $10 \div 4 = 2.5$ and $3.75 \div 1.5 = 2.5$; the corresponding sides have the same scale factor of enlargement, so the shapes are similar.

2 Surface area = 184 cm²   Volume = 160 cm³

Fluency

1

Linear scale factor	Area scale factor	Volume scale factor
3	9	27
5	25	125
4	16	64
10	100	1000
5.5	30.25	166.375

2 a) Rosie. The linear scale factor from A to B is calculated by $1.5 \div 12 = \frac{1}{8}$
  b) 64

3 a) 4   **b)** 16   **c)** 64   **d)** 67 200 mm³

Further

1 $5 \div \sqrt{6.25} = 2$

2 $2000 \div 500 = 4$
$21 \times \sqrt[3]{4} = 33.3$ cm

3 $11\,250 \div 1800 = 6.25$
Length scale factor = $\sqrt{6.25} = 2.5$
Volume scale factor = $2.5^3 = 15.625$
$3000 \div 15.625 = 192$ mm³

4 Area scale factor = $1632 \div 340 = 4.8$
Volume scale factor = $2400 \div 500 = 4.8$
The cylinders are not similar as the area scale factor and the volume scale factor are the same.

Pages 88–89
4.7 3-D Trigonometry
Foundations

1 6.9 cm

2 45.6°

Fluency

1 ADB   HBD   BDF   CGA

2 a) $\sqrt{274}$ **b)** 20.4 cm   **c)** 54.1°

3 a) 2.1 m   **b)** 35°

4 13.7 cm

Further

1 $50 \tan 30 = 28.867\ldots$ cm
$\sqrt{50^2 + 80^2} = 94.339\ldots$ cm
$\tan^{-1}\left(\frac{28.867\ldots}{94.339\ldots}\right) = 17.013\ldots$
SQT ≈ 17.0°

2 $\sqrt{9^2 + 9^2} = 12.727\ldots$
$12.727\ldots \div 2 = 6.363\ldots$ cm
$6.363\ldots \tan 75 = 23.756\ldots$ cm
$\frac{1}{3} \times 81 \times 23.756\ldots = 641.266\ldots$
≈ 640 cm³

Pages 90–91
4.8 Sine rule
Foundations

  a) $x = 44.4°$ **b)** $y = 6.62$ **c)** $a = 8.82$

Fluency

1 a) $x = 11.3$ cm   **b)** $y = 5.06$ m

2 a) $a = 66.5°$ **b)** $b = 57.1°$

3 8.6 cm

4 61.1°

Further

1 a) You can use the angle sum of the triangle to find the third angle is 40°
  b) 7.3 cm

2 $\frac{\sin A}{a} = \frac{\sin B}{b}$ gives $\sin B = 1.27\ldots$ and the sine of an angle is always less than 1

3 $\frac{\sin A}{a} = \frac{\sin B}{b}$ gives $\sin B = 0.347\ldots$ so B could be 20.3° leading to $C = 149.7°$ or B could be 159.7° leading to $C = 10.3°$

Pages 92–93
4.9 Cosine rule and choosing the rule
Foundations

  a) $a = 8.62$ **b)** $A = 38.9°$

Fluency

1 6.93 cm

2 102°

3 a) $x = 11.3$ m   **b)** $y = 94.1$ mm

4 a) $g = 44.7°$ **b)** $h = 34.6°$

5 FG = 6.73 cm

6 Perimeter = 18.8 cm

Further

1 $\frac{WY}{\sin 73} = \frac{55}{\sin 21}$
$WY = \frac{55}{\sin 21} \times \sin 73 = 146.767\ldots$ mm
$21\,540.69 = 15\,925 - 14\,700 \cos A$
$14\,700 \cos A = -5615.69$
Angle WXY = 112°

2 $90.25 = 72 - 72 \cos A$
$72 \cos A = -18.25$
Angle XOY = 104.7°

3 $5^2 = (y-1)^2 + (2y)^2 - (2 \times (y-1) \times 2y \times \cos 60$
$25 = y^2 - 2y + 1 + 4y^2 - 2y^2 + 2y$
$3y^2 - 24 = 0$
$3y^2 = 24$
$y = 2\sqrt{2}$

Pages 94–95
4.10 Area of a general triangle

Foundations

1 $a = 6.67$ **2** $\theta = 48.6°$

Fluency

1 a) 10.5 m²   **b)** 2.11 cm² or 211 mm²   **c)** 23.8 cm²

2 34.4 m²

3 a) $x = 16$ cm   **b)** $\theta = 68°$

4 86.95 cm²

Further

1 Area $= \frac{1}{2}ab\sin C$

$30 = \frac{1}{2} \times x \times x \sin 115$

$60 = x^2 \sin 115$

$\dfrac{60}{\sin 115} = x^2$

$x = \sqrt{\dfrac{60}{\sin 115}} = 8.14$ cm

2 Area of triangle $= \frac{1}{2}ab\sin C = \frac{1}{2} \times 6 \times 6 \times \sin 55 =$ 14.7447... cm²

Area of sector $= \frac{55}{360}\pi \times 6^2 = 17.2788...$ cm²

Area of shaded region $= 17.2788... - 14.7447... = 2.53$ cm²

Pages 96–97
4.11 Vector proof

Foundations

1 $\begin{pmatrix} 3 \\ -2 \end{pmatrix}$

2 $3\mathbf{p} + 2\mathbf{q}$

Fluency

1 a) $-\mathbf{b}$ **b)** $\mathbf{b}$ **c)** $-\frac{1}{2}(\mathbf{a} + \mathbf{b})$

   d) $\mathbf{a} - \mathbf{b}$ **e)** $\frac{1}{2}(\mathbf{a} - \mathbf{b})$ **f)** $-\frac{1}{2}(\mathbf{a} + \mathbf{b})$

2 a) $\mathbf{z}$ **b)** $\mathbf{x} + \mathbf{z}$ **c)** $\frac{1}{5}(\mathbf{x} + \mathbf{z})$ **d)** $-\frac{4}{5}(\mathbf{x} + \mathbf{z})$

3 $\overrightarrow{OX} = \overrightarrow{OA} + \frac{2}{5}\overrightarrow{AB} = 3\mathbf{a} + \frac{2}{5}(5\mathbf{b} - 3\mathbf{a})$

$\overrightarrow{OX} = \frac{10\mathbf{b}}{5} + \frac{9\mathbf{a}}{5} = \frac{1}{5}(9\mathbf{a} + 10\mathbf{b})$

$k = \frac{1}{5}$

Further

1 a)   **i)** $\mathbf{r} + \mathbf{s}$ **ii)** $\mathbf{s}$ **iii)** $\mathbf{s} - \mathbf{r}$

   b) $\overrightarrow{NR} = \overrightarrow{NS} + \overrightarrow{SR} = 3\mathbf{r} - \mathbf{s}$

$\overrightarrow{PR} = \overrightarrow{PO} + \overrightarrow{OR} = -\frac{1}{3}\mathbf{s} + \mathbf{r} = \mathbf{r} - \frac{1}{3}\mathbf{s}$

$\overrightarrow{NR} = 3\overrightarrow{PR}$ ($\overrightarrow{NR}$ is a multiple of $\overrightarrow{PR}$)

Therefore, $\overrightarrow{NR}$ and $\overrightarrow{PR}$ are parallel and share a common point R, so N, P and R must lie on the same line.

2 $\overrightarrow{MC} = \overrightarrow{MF} + \overrightarrow{FC} = \frac{1}{2}\mathbf{a} - 2\mathbf{b} = \frac{1}{2}(\mathbf{a} - 4\mathbf{b})$

$\overrightarrow{XC} = \overrightarrow{XF} + \overrightarrow{FC} = \frac{2}{3}\mathbf{a} - \frac{2}{3}\mathbf{b} - 2\mathbf{b} = \frac{2}{3}\mathbf{a} - \frac{2}{3}\mathbf{b} - \frac{6}{3}\mathbf{b}$

$\overrightarrow{XC} = \frac{2}{3}\mathbf{a} - \frac{8\mathbf{b}}{3} = \frac{2}{3}(\mathbf{a} - 4\mathbf{b})$

Therefore, $\overrightarrow{MC}$ and $\overrightarrow{XC}$ are parallel and the points X, M and C lie on the same line because both go through C.

Pages 98–99
5F1 Probability

Equivalent fractions or decimals are acceptable throughout the answers for this unit.

Practice

1 a) $\frac{6}{36} = \frac{1}{6}$ **b)** $\frac{18}{36} = \frac{1}{2}$ **c)** $\frac{12}{36} = \frac{1}{3}$

2 a) 0.16   **b)** 0.78

3 98

4 a) 120

   b) The relative frequency of heads is 0.54, which is close to one half, so the coin is probably fair.

5 a)

	French	Spanish	German	Total
Year 10	15	36	21	72
Year 11	28	9	11	48
Total	43	45	32	120

   b) i) $\frac{45}{120}$ **ii)** $\frac{21}{120}$ **iii)** $\frac{9}{48}$

6 a) $\frac{6}{35}$ **b)** $\frac{10}{35}$

7 $\frac{1}{216}$

8 a)

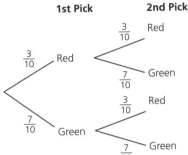

   b) $\frac{42}{100} = \frac{21}{50}$

Pages 100–101
5F2 Statistical diagrams

Practice

1

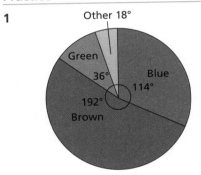

2

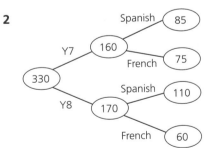

3 a)

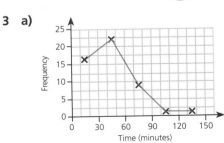

b)

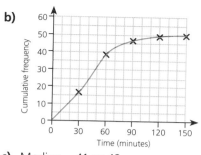

c) Median = 41 or 42
Lower quartile = 25
Upper quartile = 56
Interquartile range = 56 − 25 = 31

d)

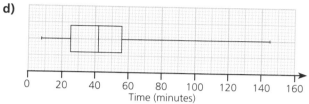

Pages 102–103
5.1 Conditional probability

Equivalent fractions or decimals are acceptable throughout the answers for this unit.

Foundations

a) $\frac{1}{3}$ **b)** 0   **c)** $\frac{7}{12}$ **d)** $\frac{3}{4}$

Fluency

1 a) $\frac{5}{10}$ **b)** $\frac{5}{9}$

2 a) $\frac{20}{40}$ **b)** $\frac{7}{19}$

3 a)

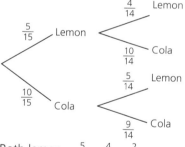

b) Both lemon = $\frac{5}{15} \times \frac{4}{14} = \frac{2}{21}$

4 a)

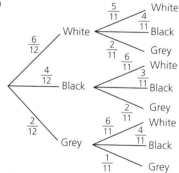

b) Same colour:
WW = $\frac{5}{22}$, BB = $\frac{1}{11}$, GG = $\frac{1}{66}$
Total = $\frac{1}{3}$

Further

1 2 followed by 4 = $\frac{1}{8} \times \frac{1}{7} = \frac{1}{56}$
3 followed by 3 = $\frac{3}{8} \times \frac{2}{7} = \frac{6}{56}$
4 followed by 2 = $\frac{1}{8} \times \frac{1}{7} = \frac{1}{56}$
Total = $\frac{8}{56}$

2 a)

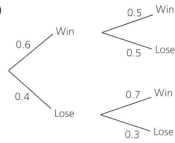

b) WL = 0.3, LW = 0.28
Total = 0.58

3 First R: $\frac{x}{x+4}$ Second R: $\frac{x-1}{x+3}$
RR = $\frac{1}{3}$
$\frac{x}{x+4} \times \frac{x-1}{x+3} = \frac{1}{3}$
$x(x-1) = \frac{1}{3}(x+3)(x+4)$
$x^2 - x = \frac{1}{3}(x^2 + 7x + 12)$
$3(x^2 - x) = x^2 + 7x + 12$

Rearrange and solve to get $x = 6$ or $x = -1$. Number of counters cannot be negative, so there were 6 red counters and 4 blue. Total = 10 counters

Pages 104–105
5.2 Histograms

Foundations

4, 5, 6, 7, 8, 9 and 10

Fluency

1 Frequency densities are 0.48, 1, 1.25, 2.2 and 0.6

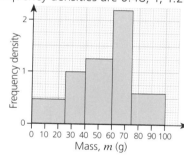

2 Frequency densities are 0.2, 0.225, 0.15, 0.16, 0.12

a)

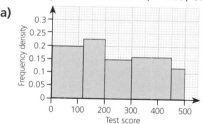

b) 49–50 students

3 a) Frequencies are 12, 18, 20 and 12   **b)** 22

Further

1 Frequencies are 30, 40 and 12

2 a) Frequency densities are 4, 6, 5

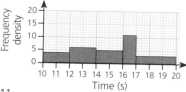

b) 11

Index